PRAISE FOR *LISTEN UP!*

"Listening with authentic intent gets results. Karen has lived it in her career. Now she has written an accessible and real book that can be used again and again. Leading with questions, locking in on values, and meeting your customers where they are at are just a few takeaways from this riveting read. A must for every conscious leader."

—**Sean Magennis,** COO, Young Presidents Organization (YPO)

"Karen Mangia clearly and powerfully articulates the significant benefits of cultivating a *Listen Up!* company culture. As a former chief customer officer and CMO, I can clearly see how businesses can build long-lasting customer relationships and advocacy by following this brilliant blueprint."

—**Vala Afshar,** Chief Digital Evangelist, Salesforce

"The most powerful strategy for creating trust and lasting relationships is intimacy. The best way to gain intimacy is to care enough to give someone your full focus and listen. REALLY listen. The superpower in business is caring, and *Listen Up!* is a practical, tactical guide to real and improved customer experience."

—**S. Anthony Iannarino,** writer, speaker, and author
of *The Only Sales Guide You'll Ever Need*

"Customer perception is everything. *Listen Up!* enables you to query, explore, and act on new and surprisingly valuable dimensions of customer perception."

—**Peter E. Cohan,** author, *Great Demo!*

Listen UP!

Listen UP!

How to Tune In to Customers and Turn Down the Noise

KAREN MANGIA

WILEY

For general information on our other products and services or for technical support, please contact our Customer Care Department within the United States at (800) 762-2974, outside the United States at (317) 572-3993 or fax (317) 572-4002.

Wiley publishes in a variety of print and electronic formats and by print-on-demand. Some material included with standard print versions of this book may not be included in e-books or in print-on-demand. If this book refers to media such as a CD or DVD that is not included in the version you purchased, you may download this material at http://booksupport.wiley.com. For more information about Wiley products, visit www.wiley.com.

Library of Congress Cataloging-in-Publication Data is available:

ISBN 9781119642114 (Hardcover)
ISBN 9781119723868 (ePDF)
ISBN 9781119723875 (ePub)

Cover Design and Illustration: Wiley
Author Image: © Rogue Images Photography.

Printed in the United States of America

SKY10020925_090220

*To my grandfather—my most cherished
mentor in business and in life*

Contents

Foreword

When I started out in business late in the 1970s, we were all working off an industrial playbook, where product was king, and capital was the scarce ingredient in the economic equation. Information technology was having a revolutionary impact on improving the efficiency of the supply chain and the back office. The big disruption was the Internet, enabling global outsourcing which, in turn, drove down the costs of products and services dramatically while simultaneously fueling a rising middle class in China, India, and other heretofore underdeveloped economies. By the end of the 20th century, we were giving ourselves high fives—mission accomplished!

Then, at the beginning of this century, a second technology revolution began to unfold around consumer applications enabled by cloud computing and mobile smartphones. Digital communication went from being an elite medium, to a commonplace experience, and finally to a de facto standard—all in the space of a couple of decades. Digital transformation is reengineering our enterprise value chains end to end. We now live in a world where access to products, and all of the information about them, is ubiquitous. We also are living in a world where taking title to products is being displaced by subscription models and as-a-service transactions. Product, in other words, is no longer king. Now it is the customer who is the scarce ingredient in the economic equation.

And that is what has led to this book.

In the Age of the Customer, every enterprise must reengineer its processes to be "customer first." That means reframing functions like Customer Support as Customer Success. It also means reorienting sales calls from presentation plus demo to provocation plus dialogue. It means focusing our products and services on outcomes, not just on deliverables. We need to secure adoption, not just ownership. We need to get inside the minds of the customers to make sure that we are addressing the things about which they really care deeply.

Marketing is no longer about what we say. Instead, it begins with what we hear. Then it must translate what we hear into what we do. That, in turn, will ultimately translate into what other people say about us. Sure, we still have our taglines and positioning statements. But now, more than ever, we have to walk the talk—we have to show that we are listening, that we do care, and that we can respond. And that means we have to listen up.

How can we listen better? For many a spouse, that can pose a lifelong challenge. Think how much more challenging it is, then, to institutionalize listening across an entire enterprise. That, in essence, is what the Age of the Customer demands, and it is precisely here then why this book can be of such great help. As an executive at Salesforce, Karen has had a front-row seat in the company that perfected the customer success function, that has lived the as-a-service mission from day one, and that has learned how dependent a land-and-expand sales model is upon customer satisfaction and retention.

Since I wrote *Crossing the Chasm: Marketing and Selling Technology Products to Mainstream Customers* (HarperCollins, 1991), I've been watching companies succeed and fail in the face of disruption, digitalization, and more. Now, in the midst of millions of messages, creating new impact requires that we listen in new ways.

Salesforce enables companies to prioritize customers unlike anyone else in the marketplace. I discovered that commitment to innovation firsthand in my work on *Zone to Win: Organizing to Compete in an Age of Disruption* (Diversion Publishing, 2015). And the companies in this book are demonstrating how to put best practices into action. No matter what industry you're in, clinging to past paradigms isn't going to build your future.

Karen has created the guidebook for leaders who are ready to listen to the voice that matters most. This book delivers a customer-focused message with clarity and precision, demonstrating that the value of your business is tied directly to the customers that you serve. Did you hear that? That's why the Age of the Customer demands your attention: It's the lifeblood of your business.

This book will show you how to tune in and tune up the most important connections in your organization. When it comes to innovation, transformation, and adding value, Salesforce gets it—and so does Karen. Read this book and you'll see why.

Geoffrey Moore, February 2020
Author of *Crossing the Chasm* and *Zone to Win*

CHAPTER 1

The Breakdown Before the Breakthrough

I was afraid.

The needle mark in my arm was still fresh, stinging from yet another blood test. My bare feet dangled off the side of the examination table. My purse sat on the floor beside my backpack, unzipped and bursting with unfinished work. I had come here to learn what was wrong, but I didn't know if I could handle the answer. Nearly four years of poking, prodding, testing, and trials had brought me into this too-bright room with turquoise shelves, where glass jars held tongue depressors and eight-inch Q-tips underneath an inspirational poster of an eagle. The long-haired man in the white lab coat held a manila folder in his hands. The pen in his pocket matched the silver color of his hair. On a single page, just outside of my view, was my fate. My future. My fear.

"We know what's wrong, and this last blood test will confirm it," my doctor said. He closed the folder and looked straight at me. "And we are going to get this fixed."

I took a deep breath. I had spent most of my thirties in the middle of a health crisis. I had watched myself gain weight, lose energy, experience symptoms of jaundice and hair loss—all without any answers as to the cause. Strange lumps in my neck were a constant unsolved mystery. The variety of medications that surrounded the sink in my bathroom had only given me new symptoms, adverse reactions, and lots of questions. I wasn't getting better. Nothing worked. So far, five doctors had failed to give me anything close to a concrete diagnosis. But today was different.

On this day, everything changed.

"I've developed a plan of treatment," Dr. Logan explained to me. "We're going to get your life back. It's going to take some time, but at least we know what we're fighting. And what we need to do to win."

As the world has faced off against the threat of the coronavirus, I can't help but be reminded of my own personal battle. A mysterious disease had me in its clutches. Luckily for me, it wasn't COVID-19. But is there any such thing as a "good" health crisis? Is one life-threatening disease more favorable than another? Unfortunately, life doesn't allow us to choose what we get. We only get to choose how we react.

I was battling against an unseen and unknown foe. Teams of doctors were confused; what they called diagnoses seemed to me to be just guesswork. Dysfunction and disappointment had led me here to a holistic doctor. Dr. Logan was as fluent in ancient Eastern healing as he was in modern medicine. When he found what others couldn't, he gave me my life back.

I wrote about my personal health journey in detail in my first book, *Success With Less*. Suffice it to say that, as a child, I had somehow contracted pesticide poisoning. Growing up in Southern Indiana, we were always outdoors. I don't know where I encountered the unnamed chemical, but it lay dormant until I entered my thirties. Then the poison woke up with a vengeance.

The journey back to health wasn't easy. At least I knew what I needed to do. I was facing the future with a new understanding. Finally, I had a plan and a path forward.

On that day, I knew I was never going back.

On that day, I discovered the power inside a horrible disease. Sounds strange, doesn't it?

On that day, I discovered how a breakdown can lead to a breakthrough.

As we face the repercussions of COVID-19, business leaders are wondering what lies ahead. We all are. Organizations have to reevaluate, reconstruct, and reprioritize. How can you care for your company, customers, and employees and find a way forward?

That's where I know I can help: because I've had to battle back from more than one setback. And I've helped thousands of companies around the world do the same.

HOW DO I MANAGE THIS CRISIS?

The first step toward getting back to health was perhaps the most vital. I had to listen—listen to the resources that could help me most. Because, when I knew what I needed to do, the real healing could begin. The doctor had given me great feedback. Now I had to use it.

In my case, my soft-spoken doctor was the voice that brought me to hear what I so desperately needed. Dr. Logan was the voice of reason and understanding—a perspective that proved to be my solution. When it was time to move forward, it was time to listen up. He pointed me toward my own resourcefulness, expanding my knowledge in a way that transformed my lifestyle. And my life.

What seemed impossible, elusive, and hidden was now revealed. Discovered. Expanded.

Have you ever had that moment when you learn something new, and you know you're never going back to the way it was before? That even if you revisit a familiar place, you know it's not the same and neither are you? When I saw the path forward—the path to health—I knew I would never be the same.

Today, as I reflect back on my battle to eliminate this poison, there's one thing I know for certain: what's past has passed. In business as in life, things follow a similar path.

A crisis forces us to pause. To prioritize. To rethink our surroundings and solutions so that we can find a way forward. Have you been there? I think we all have. I think that life has asked us all to pause and prioritize. But how do we do that in a way that's going to lead us back to professional and organizational health so that we don't just survive—rather, we thrive?

You have to listen to the people who can help you most. You have to tune in to the voice that will help you to find your future. I'm not talking about trying out a new doctor or talking to yourself during quarantine.

I'm talking about turning to resources that know what you don't know and that see what you can't see—resources that have exactly what you need (even if it's difficult to hear) during a time of crisis.

Healing begins with listening—listening to your customer.

Your customer wants to know how to find success—hopefully, via your products and services. Leading a remote workforce, driving new customer experiences, and capturing customer success. Your clients want to know how to do these things and many others, as they are striving to find their path to financial health.

I wonder: Do your customers know that they have an expert guide who's invested in their journey? I wrote this book so that they will have just that—so that you can be that guide, and so that you will know, in no uncertain terms, how to listen up more effectively, actively, and deeply than ever before. Because coming out of this crisis demands a new course of action. A treatment plan, if you will, that begins with the way that you treat your customers.

RECOVERY AND RESILIENCE

When I was sick, my mind was writing checks my body couldn't cash. I wondered:

- How do I manage through this crisis, when I don't even know what "manage" means right now or the exact extent of this crisis?

- How do I reprioritize my life?
- What can I keep, what can I discard, and what am I terrified to lose?
- How do I keep up with customer calls, meetings, and the day-to-day requirements of life?

Have you been there? As a result of my illness, I was out of energy. But thankfully, I wasn't out of options. And neither are you.

Your customer needs you. Can you hear that?

The products and services your customers need, right now and tomorrow, are waiting for you to discover. Are you listening? The future belongs to those who align and connect in more powerful ways. To hear and respond in ways that others don't. Or won't. Or can't.

SERVING AT A HIGHER LEVEL

Inside this book, you will explore the source of true recovery, resilience, and revenues. You'll take concepts like "customer success," "live listening," and "voice of the customer" to a new level—the level of healing, prosperity, and growth. I'll share proven and time-tested strategies that have helped thousands of companies from Birmingham to Brisbane and back again. We'll look at the strategies of international giants as well as the neighborhood merchants whom you've never heard of—but you will. Along the way, I'll share access to thought leaders who are innovating in the face of adversity.

Each chapter will point you toward practical and tactical advice: ideas that you can implement right away to change your results. These strategies are called "C-Sparks," and they are designed to ignite your creativity, innovation, and connection to the one source of wellness in a transformed world.

Together, we will reveal what my doctor gave to me: Clarity. Direction. Guidance. And a new path forward.

THE BREAKDOWN LEADS TO A BREAKTHROUGH

Through these pages and chapters, you'll learn how to ask better questions, take ego out of the conversation, build greater alignment, and add value to your company's bottom line. You will find the changes that you need to make and which your customers crave. Because listening is everyone's job. And the only way forward is together.

When you have a *Listen Up!* organization, you win as a team—often, as a team of teams. An organization that listens up understands that connecting with customers isn't just the job of a particular division, sector, or service squad. Working remotely can still mean that we're working together. Listening means building a community—a community that can stand and expand on the culture inside your organization, to shift the hearts and minds of the people who support it.

At Google, here's how they describe their customer experience team:

1. There is no single research group.
2. There is no single research role.
3. There is no single research process.[1]

What could that kind of alignment and understanding mean to you and your company? More importantly, to your customers? It's time to find out.

Ultimately, a *Listen Up!* organization will deliver shared value. Shared success, because our focus in these pages is on growth. But from where, exactly, is that growth going to come?

I will share with you the answer that is true, but only 100 percent of the time: growth comes from your customers. If you're wondering how your business will recover and thrive, that's another great question.

Better ask the person who holds the answers. Guess who that is?

Customer success is what drives every business today.[1] According to the *Customer Success Association* (https://www.customersuccessassociation.com/), the mission of customer success is to increase sustainable proven value for both the customers and the company. While Salesforce (https://www.salesforce.com/) didn't invent customer success (that title goes to another CRM company called Vantive, where Marie Alexander created the first Customer Success department in 1996), many believe that Salesforce perfected it. In 2005, Salesforce quickly built what has become the largest and best-known Customer Success departments in any industry, called "Customers for Life." The purpose of the group was to increase retention and adoption—words that point to profitability, service, and impact.

Here are the four pillars of Customer Success. These are ideas that we will explore in detail in the pages that follow:

1. **Technology Is the Turning Point.** Machine learning and artificial intelligence are here to stay. Success will involve using these tools to understand your customers like never before. We will focus on the strategy and intention that will help you to forge new and deeper relationships, so that

---

[1]Chapman, Chris (2018). "User Experience Research: Behavioral Science to Improve Product Experience." Presented at the Annual Convention of the American Psychological Association. San Francisco: August 2018.

you can deliver more intelligent, personalized experiences. More importantly, we will focus on the people behind the process, offering a kind of authentic intelligence to complement the artificial ones.

2. **Success Depends on Every Stakeholder.** From the interns to the C-Suite, engagement is the driver of exceptional customer success. Coach Phil Dickens at Indiana University often said, "You practice like you play." Practice taking care of your people or, as the saying goes, they will take care of you (and not in a good way). The *Listen Up!* organization works from outside in: listening to the people who matter most drives the behaviors that create results. But aren't your internal employees your customers as well? Listening to every stakeholder is putting success into practice. And playing to win.

3. **The Gap Is Shrinking.** The gap between what customers really want from business and what's actually possible is vanishing rapidly. That shift is changing everything, from expectations to possibilities. The future isn't about learning to be better at doing what we already do. It's about how far we can stretch the boundaries of our imagination. You might even say our genius. The ability to produce success stories that weren't possible a few years ago to help customers thrive in dramatic new ways is what's going to become a driver of growth for any successful company. The gap between what's possible and what's available is getting smaller every day. Meanwhile, what's getting bigger and bigger? Customer expectations.

4. **Wanted—Miracle Workers.** I believe that we're entering a new age in which customers will demand miracles from you. Whether you make cars, solar panels, television programs, or anything else, opportunities for modern-day miracles are everywhere. Sound far-fetched? So was penicillin, once upon a time. As Eleanor Roosevelt famously said, "The future belongs to those who create it." Innovation is the only way forward—blazing new trails to meet new expectations. We have to resist the urge to make quick marginal improvements and spend more time listening deeply to what customers really want, even if they're not fully aware of it yet. In the end, you can make miracles happen, especially when you see that customer success is built on connection.

Today we sit at an inflection point. We find ourselves at the intersection of "too much information" and "what really matters." What you've done before and what got you to this point isn't going to get you (and your customers) where you need to go. It's time to make the right turn.

We need a new map—a better GPS—for the road ahead.

This book will give you the tools to engage your entire organization in developing possibilities. You will see new connections. Ask better questions. Lead your teams (and your customers) to powerful new results. And discover that everyday miracles are within your grasp.

Every company approaches listening in its own way. I can't guess what you might spend on your customer experience, but I can tell you the exact cost of doing nothing.

Half-measures and poor execution are two things that you can't afford, no matter what your balance sheet says. Ignore the voice of the customer, and you will bankrupt your organization.

There is a way forward—for you and for your team. The cure is here, right in front of you, but it takes time. Commitment. I can tell you from my own experience. To get through a crisis, you've got to turn to the one resource that can help you most. In business, that means listening for the answers that will guide your future. A new experience—and a new way of looking at customer success—is in your hands, right now. You don't have to wait for a breakthrough. The journey has already begun.

CHAPTER 2

Don't Bet on Your Blind Spots

Ashley Revell is the typical guy next door. Average height. Average weight. Average amount of hair. Gainfully employed with a modest savings account. Single and seeking. One day, he had a drink with some friends, and Ashley decided to break the rules. That was when a happy-hour dare turned him from pub patron to gutsy gambler.

"*Wouldn't it be great,*" his friends asked him, "*if we went to Las Vegas ... and bet everything on one spin?*"

The ultimate bet. The gambler's dream. The big payoff.

Through the cloudy haze of beers and bravado, this intriguing inquiry captured Ashley's attention in a way that was far from average. As he thought about the idea of betting it all, adrenaline found him quickly—like a tenacious tiger pursuing its prey.

Ashley wondered: "*What If?*"

HOW "WHAT IF?" BECAME, "WHY NOT?"

Ashley inventoried his assets. Just over $15,000 in savings. A used BMW in pretty good shape. He still had his Rolex. Golf clubs. What did he have to lose? he wondered. Curiously, "everything" was not the first thought to cross his mind.

"*At pretty much every stage, everyone I knew said it was just a stupid thing to do. My [mother] obviously said it was a silly idea and that I should be settling down. My father was exactly the same,*" he recalled.

He didn't listen to their advice. Over the next six months, Ashley sold all of his possessions. Reasoning would only slow him down at this point, so he didn't have time for it. He was on an adventure—determined to reject average.

He boarded his high-stakes flight to Las Vegas in a rented tuxedo, paid for with the money he earned when he sold all of his clothes.

Ashley stepped onto the bright, plush carpet at the Plaza Casino and Hotel. Rehearsed and ready, with an entourage and photographers in tow, he felt almost famous.

The cashier raised an eyebrow when she saw the crew and the cameras approaching the cash cage. She shook her head as she methodically transformed Ashley's life savings—now $135,000—into 14 rows of neatly stacked chips. Each clink of the plastic chips reminiscent of the clink of the pint glasses nearby. Ashley looked down at the stacks of chips, his lifetime achievements placed meticulously on the red velvet in front of him.

Intent on his mission, Ashley ignored the smell of musky cologne and wafting tobacco residue as he stepped away from the cashier. Carrying his life in his hands, he stepped forward to find the roulette table that would determine his future.

At the table, one glaring question punctured the brief and sudden silence: "*Red or black?*"

Ashley gingerly placed the chips on the table. He took a deep breath as he pushed his future toward the croupier.

"*When I spin the ball, if it goes around more than three times before you say red or black, it's a 'no' bet,*" said the man behind the wheel.

Months of planning and execution had numbed him to what was at stake. His eyes focused on a single square with a single number. His number. His big success. Or his big regret. Which would it be . . . ?

Would you be willing to bet your business—or your career—on a single number?

Unlikely.

Yet thousands of businesses (and CEOs) gamble the future on a daily basis by going all in on Net Promoter Score (NPS). They're playing a high-stakes game of chance based on a single number. Are you? Like corporate croupiers, these leaders ask customers one self-administered question: "How likely are you to recommend our business, based on your recent experience?"

Then the real gambling begins.

In 2018, NPS was cited more than 150 times in earnings conference calls by 50 S&P 500 companies, according to a *Wall Street Journal* analysis of transcripts. Compared with the same organizations from five years earlier, that's more than four times as many mentions—a 400 percent increase in NPS chatter! In five years, nearly *three times* as many companies were focused on this single number, according to transcript analysis.

The same study went on to discover dozens of public companies also report NPS scores in securities filings, even tying NPS results to employee compensation. So, is that a fair bet?

A growing number of companies are going all in on a single square.

Like Ashley Revell, these organizations are betting the house on a single number.

How do you think that's going to turn out? (By the way, if you're interested in the outcome of Ashley's sensational spin, visit karenmangia.com /biggamble.)

Are you the Ashley Revell of your C-Suite, with all of your company's assets riding on an outcome that you're unable to predict and unlikely to sustain?

- Red or black
- Promoter or detractor
- Place your bets
- Are the odds really in your favor?

This corporate roulette game isn't the same. The house almost never wins, because NPS is a bad bet for everybody involved. When the results are revealed, how equipped are you and your senior leaders to discern the answers to these mission-critical questions:

- Why do you win?
- Why do you lose?
- How do you influence, sustain, or change that outcome?

The Challenge: We're asking the wrong questions—and we're asking the wrong questions of the wrong people

How often do we as human beings do what we say we're going to do? Like when the dentist asks, "Are you going to floss your teeth?"—there's really only one answer.

But is it the truth?

The doctor wants to know if you're going to eat more vegetables. Of course, you and I say yes because we only have the best intentions, right?

But intention is not action, and that's the issue with the NPS question. Asking, "How likely are you to recommend our business based on your recent experience?" is a measure of one key sentiment: likelihood. How LIKELY are you to floss? Eat better? Really do something to recommend my business?

CEO Christine Marcus discovered the dangers of asking the wrong questions of the wrong people the hard way—by losing her largest customer. Talking backstage with her at a conference in Amsterdam, I had the chance to hear her story firsthand.

Having emigrated from Egypt with her family to escape religious persecution, Christine was no stranger to hardship. Her prearranged marriage at age

17—a cultural tradition—ended in divorce. As a single mother, she needed to provide for herself and for her children. Like many female entrepreneurs, doing what had to be done was the motivation to start her own business (https://bit.ly/listenup-ChristineMarcus).

And that's exactly what she did. Christine knew two things really well: food and service. But not just serving food—she wanted to cook up something different. Something unique. A business that created delicious experiences. She built her B2B business around organizations that realize how the overall employee experience is a big part of attracting and retaining top talent.

Alchemista (https://www.alchemista.com/) is a premier corporate catering concierge service, delivering creative food and brand solutions for high-growth businesses. Her customers are, according to Christine, "elite and specific." They believe that they have to have an awesome office culture, with free meals as an employee benefit. But not just burgers and fries for her clients.

"We help companies compete with Google," she explains. "Food plus experience equals culture [for our customers], and that's where Alchemista comes in. We don't make any food—we're just really good at finding great stuff." Her company sources unique culinary choices—from fast to slow food. "And then," Christine adds, "we make everything better."

"We're never going to have thousands of customers—that's not our approach. We have a short list of clients." Hers is a subscription model, delivering onsite multiple days per week. Christine clarifies, "It's hospitality service. Not food delivery."

As Christine's business grew, her growing leadership responsibilities resulted in fewer opportunities to interact directly with customers. Like most founders, she trusted her account team with the task of *retention*. On the surface, it seemed so simple: keep customers by keeping customers *happy*.

Resting on residual relationships established earlier in her career, interspersed with occasional account team conversations, she became removed from day-to-day client contact.

For her teams, she asked just one question: "How likely are we to retain this customer?"

Ah. A single, simple ask. Sounds familiar, doesn't it?

Which do you choose: Red or black?

THE GREATEST NIGHTMARE ANY CEO CAN FACE

Christine was sitting at her desk in her Boston headquarters when an email arrived on a cloudy Friday morning. The Chief Executive at her largest customer sent her a short but stunning message.

"Thank you very much. Your service stinks. Our employees hate it. You guys are fired. Don't even bother sending anyone in on Monday."

The email sent shockwaves through Christine's body. She blinked. She looked at the header. The subject line: "Whaaaaaaaaaaaaaaat?"

How could this have happened? Where did this come from? Whatever happened to the 30-day notice in the customer agreement?

She felt her heart pounding as she instantly calculated the damages: over 50 percent of her revenue had just walked out the door.

Of course, she didn't let her initial anxiety stop her. She knew she could turn this around . . . right?

She immediately picked up the phone. Her call to the CEO was not answered—just like the next 862 calls she would make.

The CEO refused to talk to her.

Emails landed unanswered.

She had thought that, if there were unresolved problems, the CEO would call her, right? That seemed like a safe bet.

Except that it wasn't. . . . *And it never is.*

What Christine came to realize is that customers vote with their funds more often than with their feedback.

Unbeknown to her, errors had piled up and orders were late. Consistent mistakes—and a pattern of missteps—led her customer to make a single and harsh decision.

Without feedback. Without recourse. Without mercy.

Through the attempted service recovery, Christine tried everything. At first, she thought about firing her entire account team, starting with the account rep who (she assumed) was asleep at the wheel. He had been telling her that everything was fine!

Was it time for heads to roll—starting with the sleepy sales guy?

In a word: No.

As I listened to Christine tell her story, we shared a profound realization. It hit me like a ton of bricks: Every system performs perfectly for the task it was designed to do.

Christine had a process in place—a process that was generating errors and keeping communication at a distance. A process built on *lagging indicators* that was working. She was using the past to manage the present. Have you been there?

It's like trying to turn left while looking only in your rear-view mirror—you can do it, but not very well. And if there are surprises on your right—or right in front of you—you may or may not see what's coming!

The process was broken. Not the driver.

Christine realized that the culture of the organization was the problem—not the people.

The biggest error—and it was built into the system—was a belief that the client CEO would provide feedback if problems arose. Christine felt *certain* that the CEO would contact her if there were problems. Instead, he commented with his wallet—he closed it.

"Hurt people holler."
                              Van Jones, author of Beyond the Messy Truth

As you can imagine, this disastrous departure hit her business hard. Even though she was hemorrhaging cash—or maybe because of it—she couldn't afford to fix the wrong thing. Can you?

What Christine discovered painfully (and publicly) is that one unhappy customer can poison all of the others. Boston is a tight-knit community. The departed CEO wouldn't talk to Christine, but he was talking to all of his C-Suite friends. Big complaints in a small world meant that Alchemista had a lot more to lose.

Christine decided to blow up the process and create a culture around what was really missing—customer feedback. Her work was really just beginning—culture doesn't change overnight. As the attrition of customers spread, she took a hard look at what she could have done differently. If only she had asked better questions, she thought.

If only she had asked the *right* questions. Of the *right* people. At the *right* time.

If only.

Never Again

"I made a commitment to never have that same sinking, crappy feeling of being completely slapped in the face," she stated. "Direct, unfiltered feedback from every customer we have, no matter how large we get, is my resolve. That mistake I made . . . ," she says, her voice trailing off. She looked at the floor, recalling the memory of the error. Was there more than one? With conviction in her voice, she stated without hesitation, "If we had the right customer feedback program in place, that disaster never would have happened."

She implemented tools to provide real-time feedback using some of the questioning ideas you'll see in an upcoming chapter. An innovative, real-time survey solution opened the company up to new possibilities, closing off the "gotchas" that had punished her in the past. She began reading every customer response personally. Then those customer responses were sent to everyone in the company.

Today, Christine has a robust customer listening and measurement program that fosters awareness, engagement, and transparency. She's broken down the barriers between the C-Suite and the customer. Her business thrives in Boston, Washington, D.C., and New York City.

But beyond the growth, she's built something else that few companies ever achieve: an enviable 100 percent customer retention rate. Get that—100 percent retention. She's committed to keeping her customers, and they are just as committed to her.

> "I don't know what our NPS score is," she says, frankly. "And I don't care. What matters is we have a 100 percent retention rate. And our business has grown, in every account, over the last 18 months."

What would a result like that mean to you and your company?
(See Christine tell her story on YouTube: http://bit.ly/TheAlchemistaStory.)

Are you willing to do what it takes to retain 100 percent of your customers?

"Yes! Of course!" you're screaming. "Who answers no to a question like that?" I'm guessing you have the best intentions.

Ready to move from intention to action? Here's how!

C-Sparks: Ideas to Ignite Innovation

You don't have to lose your largest client, as Alchemista did, to transform the way you listen to your customers. Nobody needs to get ambushed into action. But without a plan for listening, you can expect some unpleasant surprises.

These three strategies will help your C-Suite manage risk, unlock opportunities, and improve employee engagement.

1. **Drop the Veil**
   a. *Are you really ready to look at your customer, even if she's not smiling?* Don't settle for good intentions! Good intentions are nice, but the best leaders have something else: they have good *agreements*. What is the agreement that you, as the senior leader, need to gain before the meeting really begins? The agreement centers on the team's focus: everyone's need to look past the veil, go beyond intentions, and really listen to the voice of the customer. (You'll learn more about this in Chapter 11, "Dealing with Disruption.")

(continued)

(continued)

   b. ***Step 1: You have to take time to get clear, vulnerable, and real about your commitment to listening in new ways.*** And remember, just because you say something and heads nod doesn't mean that you have agreement, boss. (Check out Chapter 10, "The Secret Sauce.")

   c. ***Make sure that you get verbal buy-in, and have it articulated right up front.*** Why? Because agreement builds accountability. If you are in charge, and you are committed to hearing what needs to be said, make sure that everyone else is ready for the unvarnished truth. It's a funny thing: what you speak into the room often appears—and that's what's needed, now more than ever, in every conversation where the customer is being discussed. (Want to learn more about revealing your genius? Head to Chapter 8, "Got Genius?")

   d. ***Gain agreement around willingness to listen.*** What would that look like for your team? Ask for verbal or written agreement or both. Get people to say what they are going to do—in front of everyone. Drop the veil. Make a vow. Pick up on the conversation. (See Chapter 7, "Better Questions, Better Answers.")

2. Put It on the Wall

   a. ***Assess senior leadership alignment.*** In your next staff meeting, give each one of your senior leaders three Post-it® Notes. Ask each person to provide answers to these three questions and have them post their responses on the wall with no conversation, no comparisons, no Googling, and no copying! (*Spoiler alert*: *Responses may vary wildly.*)

   QUESTION #1: What is the primary reason customers choose us over our competitors?

   EXTRA CREDIT: Pick one specific customer. Start with the one you dislike the most and have everyone focus there. Once you get the hang of this exercise, you can introduce another specific competitor, and another. Specifics are important if you want specific answers!

   QUESTION #2: What is the primary reason why customers choose our competitor over us?

   QUESTION #3: What are the biggest surprises that you see? Discuss the discoveries—and the disconnects! What did you uncover? What new information was revealed?

EXTRA CREDIT BONUS ROUND: Do the same exercise with execs and frontline employees (or supervisors) in the same room. Choose a specific competitor. Compare answers. On a whiteboard, write out the biggest differences, and look for things that show up more than once.

In my customer experience workshops, where I unite the top tier with the front line, we explore these differences and observations. We are always identifying areas for action and gaining new levels of commitment into the places where change is needed. How about you? (The Genius Question is revealed in Chapter 8—check it out!)

3. Invite the Customer to Center Stage

Reach out to customers who don't renew. Connect with some folks who don't necessarily like you. Find a former customer who prefers your competition. Stop guessing about why they switched. Don't believe your own branding. Don't get lost on your "powerful slogan" or mission statement, because the customer is the mission. And branding is what others say about you. Especially when "others" means people who are buying from someone else. Do you know why customers make a different choice? Do you know why because it's what you've been told . . . or is it what you've heard firsthand from someone who perhaps doesn't like your company very much? Look, I don't always like my alarm clock, but it always tells the truth. And that truth gets me where I need to be. How about you? Listen to the alarms—to the news that might be hard to hear. Because that's the sound that will get you where you need to be. (Your step-by-step guide is waiting for you in Chapter 10 where I reveal "The Secret Sauce.")

a. At Salesforce, we partner with customer-facing teams to identify customers who would be willing to provide candid feedback. These customers, once identified, are asked to share their experience in various formats. Could you do the same? Bring the voice of your customers to life by hosting a customer panel at your next Town Hall meeting, trade show, or customer event. The key is to feature customers who chose not to renew. You might have to spring for a fancy dinner in order to get people to attend. The price of pasta pales in comparison to the value in bold and courageous feedback. Then use the meeting results as an opportunity to highlight one new customer-driven priority. Or maybe that should say "competition-driven" priority?

(continued)

(continued)

    b. If you're in a leadership position, emphasize the value of feedback that challenges existing beliefs. Look for it. Explore it. And ask other members of the leadership team to do the same.

    c. What new priorities are showing up? Share anecdotes and experiences within the C-Suite and throughout every level of the organization. Future chapters will show you exactly how to spread the word—with deep-dive stories about companies who are bringing these best practices to life. (Learn more about how to create greater alignment between your company and your customers in Chapter 5, "When Organizations Are Out of Alignment.")

DECREASE DISTANCE BETWEEN YOUR HOME OFFICE AND THE C-SUITE: FIRST STEPS

Wondering how to connect your leaders to customer concerns without confronting the culture of your company? Here's a quick recipe for engagement at the executive level, so that you gain firsthand insight (and top-level buy-in) for customer listening.

Be Selective

Choose a senior leader to be a part of customer follow-up. This means that the leader you choose will be talking directly to customers. This is the antidote from the Alchemista story, and you've got to get in front of customer concerns by (wait for it) getting in front of customers. Remember, none of us is as smart as all of us. Don't let anyone's title prevent the exchange of vital information. Are you ready? Because once the first leader connects with customers, the rotation begins.

Why Stop at One?

What would happen if each one of your senior leaders contacted a customer who gave you a low score on a survey? Or failed to renew? How much insight could you gain? Until everyone at the top talks to someone on the front lines, there's still an opportunity for misunderstanding—for missing something and for making big mistakes. If the voice of the customer matters, leadership (ALL leadership) will pick up the phone to hear it. What business case and initiatives would your leadership team see firsthand? After all, if you say something's a problem, but leadership doesn't see it, does it really exist? No.

Don't explain the challenges: Ask for courageous leaders who can see and hear what's going on. Don't be afraid to cut out the middleman and get execs engaged with the conversation that matters most—what the customer is saying. And, if you're curious to know how to take ego out of the conversation, that story is waiting for you in just a few pages. Because executive buy-in is where the conversation really begins.

Outcomes from implementing these strategies include the following:

- Uncovering blind spots in your customer relationships
- Broadening and deepening your competitive intelligence
- Improving your customer renewal rate
- Deepening relationships with customers and prospects
- Increasing employee engagement and satisfaction

For additional strategies to transform the way you tune in to your customers, visit http://karenmangia.com/listenup/tune-in.

Breaking down barriers between the C-Suite and customers is the fastest way to implement the change that's needed. Stop betting on a single number and eliminate surprises by making the voice of every customer (even the ones who don't buy from you anymore) a top priority.

As it turns out, listening to the customer starts with asking the right questions. And the question that's asked in the next chapter might surprise you—almost as much as the answer does.

CHAPTER 3

The Beginner's Mindset

I'll never forget my first sales pitch.

"Don took the early retirement package," my new boss was explaining to me. He looked out over his reading glasses, while I looked over his office. Where was this conversation headed, I wondered? And who was Don?

Since I never planned to go into sales, I had never planned to go into the sales manager's office. You know that saying, "Man plans, God laughs"? I think I was waiting for the punchline.

"And so, we need you to take the lead as the account manager for a few of our customers," my new boss shared, in addition to your day job. Just until we can hire a backfill."

I was being assigned to the "STAR" account module. I soon discovered that this customer set lacked the luster and the shine the name might otherwise imply. STARs were the smallest customers: "Small, Troubled, And Risky," was what I think the acronym really implied. These accounts didn't shine brightly, because they were often located in the dustiest, darkest office parks. Moreover, their results were shoved into the dismal corners of our company's daily sales forecast.

The first glimpse of my opportunity to shine was the one customer (out of the 100 I supported) who agreed to hear my pitch.

On that hot summer day, I sat in the customer's lobby. If you could call it that. It was more like a poorly lit closet, filled with a couch, a table, six trade magazines from last year, a coffee machine, and two armless chairs. I steadied myself in the less rickety one while sipping a cup of coffee that reminded me of my favorite truck stop.

Entering the client's conference room, I slowly pulled a beige manila folder out of my borrowed briefcase—like a magician starting a trick. It was time for my first pitch.

I shared the printed proposal with the customer. I had cleverly down-loaded it from our company's intranet site. Then I proceeded to read the entire document. Out loud—word . . . for . . . word.

Can you imagine?

But get this, even with an incredibly terrible pitch, I still won the deal.

How?

Because, in spite of all of the tactics I got wrong, I got the most important strategy right.

Luckily for both of us, the proposal was short—so story time didn't go on too long. But after reading every line from the proposal, I stopped and did the most valuable thing anyone can do in front of a customer: I asked for their feedback. And I listened.

Maybe it was because I didn't have some dazzling PowerPoint to offer them. I didn't even possess a persuasive argument that stepped outside of the written word. But somehow, I knew what you do too: listening was what mattered most.

Because if I say it but the customer doesn't see it, it doesn't exist. In every sales presentation since, I've realized one thing: there are always two presentations in the room. The one that I give. And the one the customer hears. Which one do you think is most important?

Getting into the customer's world—rickety chairs and all—was where I knew I needed to be. Maybe I didn't have a great pitch, but I had some-thing more important: the beginner's mindset. I wasn't burdened with what I already knew. Instead, I was on a mission to discover what I didn't know (which was kind of everything, at this point).

I was sincerely curious. There were things I needed to know. Perhaps, most importantly, I was curious about the customer's viewpoint, because I knew it was the one that mattered most.

Getting clear on your brand message, and having a decent sales pitch if you're in sales, are valuable. But listening to the customer is priceless.

If I could point to one key factor in my success, it's been the three-step strategy that I discovered that hot summer day, in a nearly abandoned office park—**Listen > Align > Act.**

Because I only had one customer at the time, I invested countless hours asking questions: listening attentively to the answers, studying customer service case notes, and reviewing the account history. Then I aligned my actions—the fill-in-the-blank sections of the proposal template—explicitly to the customer's asks. What I discovered, as a result, is a timeless truth: **Customers invest when they feel heard.**

In my work with thousands of entrepreneurs, executives, and business leaders in the decades that followed, there's been a delicate (and sometimes impossible) balance in play. I've seen how difficult it is to scale the high-touch, personalized experiences of one customer to hundreds or thousands of employees. It's even more difficult when you have hundreds or thousands of customers to consider.

The programs that bombard execs with data are called "Voice of the Customer" (VoC). You knew that, right? Unfortunately, VoC is a title that is filled with lofty intentions and lackluster alignment. And, more often than not, it has an uncertain destination. The journey leaves executives stranded, lacking the kinds of signposts, signals, and context that can create clarity for the C-Suite.

We all know that we need to listen, but are we asking the questions that matter? I'm talking about the ones that:

- Are truly on customers' minds
- Ask customers about their business, and what success looks like from their vantage point (rather than from your company's point of view, agenda, or siloed perspective)
- Really get your entire organization closer to your customers

If your scores are high, but your profits aren't, is anybody really winning? You have to open up your organization—including the C-Suite—to listen to the customer's language. And that message has to connect to top- and bottom-line results.

If your VoC program isn't meaningful to your brand and to the valuation of your business, it's time to make a change. It's time to begin again.

The VoC journey is designed to get closer to the customer: that's the intention. The irony is that the more time execs spend with numbers, the less time they spend with customers . . . and with the stories that create the much-needed context for the data.

The programs are intended to help companies to scale customer intimacy. Instead, customers are reduced to stats that don't tell the whole story. It's about as intimate as a spreadsheet can be, I guess, though I've never had a spreadsheet buy me a glass of Chardonnay.

I'm not saying that I don't like numbers. I'm saying that I don't drink Chardonnay. But I digress.

Look, numerical details are important, but dancing with data alone is a dangerous game. Holding on to just the numbers has left many executives feeling empty-handed.

A FALSE SENSE OF SECURITY

If the customer service score moves in the right direction, does that look like winning to you? Or is your company doing a victory dance on the five-yard line—celebrating simple scores—instead of doing what it takes to win the game?

Let's face it: It's easier just to look at top-line numbers. But that's sort of like managing your business based only on top-line revenues.

There's more to the story, and this book will help you to discover it, deliver it, and see new opportunities. It's time to design a best-in-class program for your company, and here's why it matters. According to research completed by the Aberdeen Group, companies with innovative listening programs enjoy the following:

- An average revenue growth of 42.8 percent YoY (year over year)
- A 55 percent greater client retention rate
- A decrease in customer service costs by 23.6 percent YoY
- And a whopping 292 percent greater employee engagement rate

In a recent survey from Accenture (http://bit.ly/listenup-Accenture) 90 percent of company leaders believe that CX (customer experience) is important to achieving their strategic goals. Yet a whopping 80 percent don't believe that they excel at CX in a way that can drive financial results! And 72 percent admit that they have no direct influence over CX results.

PwC's most recent Annual Global CEO survey (https://bit.ly/ceo-survey-listenup) quantifies the magnitude of the gap between information that CEOs need and information that CEOs get. When asked to reflect on the information they find critical versus the extent to which they feel that they received that information in adequate form, CEOs rated data about customers' preferences and needs as 94 percent critical and only 15 percent adequate.

Barely. Adequate.

Look at those percentages again:

94 versus 15. That's not victory. That's a blowout—and your leadership team is getting killed right now.

How is that glaring gap possible when IDC reports that worldwide spending (https://bit.ly/listenup-IDCReport) on customer experience (CX) technologies exceeded $508 billion in 2019 . . . and it is projected to reach $641 billion in 2022? Companies aren't getting what they paid for, and it's time to change the game.

What senior executives secretly reveal to me every week in animated boardroom and backroom conversations is that they don't have enough confidence in the information they receive *about* their customers to make mission-critical decisions *for* their customers.

What CEOs are hesitant to reveal in public, they are relieved to reveal in private: The numbers literally do not speak for themselves.

Because numbers without context are meaningless. (Remember the old George Carlin joke, "Here's a partial score from the Notre Dame game: 11.")

Without the context and insights surrounding the numbers, the data is meaningless at worst and incomplete at best.

No wonder confidence is low—the context can't always be trusted. What would it mean to you and your organization if you knew that you were asking the right people the right questions at the right time, and gaining insight into the stories that you've been missing? What if you could truly listen, align, and act in a way that brought people together around a single, all-important goal, namely delivering the goods and services that your customers crave in a way that's easy, engaging, and profitable?

It's time to stop saying, "We are customer-focused," and start living it. How long do you want to wait to get good at this? A beginner's mindset might help you to answer that question in a way that points you toward new discoveries—the discoveries that you will find in the pages of this book.

I've coached countless leaders who have fallen prey to managing "relationships by the numbers." The intended strategy? Scale customer listening while ignoring mission-critical red flags and sidestepping opportunities to address customer concerns. How do you think that date's gonna end?

There's a connection that's missing. A connection between what customers say and what employees relay when it comes to listening. And if executives can't connect with those employees—or with those customers in a way that brings the data to life—how can leaders make effective decisions?

It's time to change these statistics—for yourself and for your company—and do it now.

LISTENING IS THE FIRST STEP IN DECISION MAKING

Successful companies understand the journey—the path from listening to understanding, from statistics to stories, from ego to empathy, and from apathy to action. What is behind those steps? A sincere curiosity and a willingness to heed the words of Mark Twain:

> It ain't what you don't know that can hurt you. It's what you think you know that just ain't so.
>
> *Mark Twain*

Sometimes, leading with experience means having the discipline to forget what you thought you knew—to treat each customer interaction as if it were the first.

Beginner's mindset or beginner's luck: In my first sales call I had the former, and it created the latter. Note that I couldn't get defensive in the face of feedback—I had nothing to defend. From a defenseless position (How often do you see that within your company?), I started working on new information and creating new results. Listening was the common thread, based on a relentless curiosity to find the right questions.

In the coming chapters, you will discover:

- How the beginner's mind can take ego out of the conversation so that hard-hitting feedback can be heard, listened to, and understood, without an atmosphere of defensiveness, disconnection, and distraction.
- Tools to unlock stranded customer value, uncover hidden meaning, and measure what matters most to your customers and to your business.
- How the VoC contributes to the value of your company, especially in times of succession, acquisition, and valuation.
- Tactics to elevate the survey, lean in to the customer story, and raise "customer success" to the level of competitive advantage.
- How to move out of the silos and design your organization as a single team aligned around the customer.

But first we have to look at the solitary question that resets the journey. It's the single question that points an entire organization toward customer alignment or restructuring. Do you know what that question is?

CHAPTER 4

Big Impact

Have you ever gone into the emergency room, either for yourself or with someone else? What are the first two questions that they ask you once you provide your insurance information and complete the required forms?

1. Are you allergic to any medications?
2. When's the last time you ate or drank something?

They ask these questions because they are trying to assess your current situation: if you pass out or need triage, or whatever the case may be, they are ready to handle the situation. So you give the person at the front desk this information. You give the requested feedback.

Then you sit and you wait. Soon, you are called in to take the next step—to come in for treatment. Someone in a lab coat comes in, and they ask you the following:

1. Are you allergic to any medications?
2. When's the last time you ate or drank something?

If this is an emergency situation, what's your first thought? It's probably not, "I love redundancy, let's take our time and go through this again." Maybe you've got a few questions of your own like, "Who's in charge here?" and "Don't you realize that I just gave you this information?" Maybe even something like, "Hey, when do you want to focus on my health and well-being and the reason why I'm in the emergency room in the first place?"

When customer listening programs are scanning existing feedback, there's so much information. Asking the same questions over and over again is the exact opposite of acting with a sense of urgency about the information that's really mission-critical.

What if the nurse approached you in the emergency room and said:

"I see here that you've been asked the same questions several times over and over again. I'm not going to do that. I want to focus on what really matters to you. Where does it hurt and what's brought you in here today?"

No surveys. Only solutions. Because now, the conversation is focused on what really matters: the patient's health.

For healthcare companies, understanding how best to serve patients is critical from a customer success standpoint. Because if you guess wrong and don't move quickly, the results can be painful. Tragic, even.

That's why asking the right questions at the right time is so vital. Crucial. Indispensable.

Christi Hill knew that asking the right questions at the right time was key to her company's success. She was on a mission: there was no time to waste in meetings debating the strategic or tactical nature of survey questions. There was a more important customer experience question—a Big Impact question—that needed to be answered.

With offices in 18 countries, Eli Lilly is a $22 billion pharmaceutical leader. Founded by a former Civil War Colonel over 150 years ago, the company has earned one of the best brand reputations in the life sciences industry (according to Biospace (https://bit.ly/listenup-BioSpace). The company made a name for itself by mass producing the polio vaccine and becoming the first company to synthesize and market human insulin. The company may best be known as one of the largest manufacturers of psychiatric medications, including Prozac and Cymbalta, as well as the antipsychotic Zyprexa (the company's best-selling medication).

Can you imagine the myriad of complexities (and customers) within their business model?

Christi Hill can. She's the customer experience strategy leader at Lilly, and she was determined to resolve a critical challenge within the multi-billion-dollar pharmaceutical giant.

The company's employees all align under this umbrella:

"Lilly unites caring with discovery to create medicines to make life better for people around the world."

The employees at Lilly are there to do big things—like treating cancer, diabetes, and autoimmune disorders—as part of improving lives. Could Christi turn this passion into deeper customer connection, innovation, and direction for the company? Or would strong passions lead to strong preconceptions, resulting in a turf war over the status quo?

If Lilly wasted time guessing about the customers and what they needed, lives were at stake. The wrong choice could mean that people would suffer, care would go undelivered, and—to be blunt—people could die.

Knowing the customer and serving the customer wasn't just mission-critical—it was the mission. Precision, urgency, and customer responsiveness: these things matter at the highest level at Lilly. But passion, if misplaced, can lead to turf wars—not customer care.

The Big Impact question is simple on the surface, but it is profound in its response. At first glance, the Big Impact question can look easy. But it's not. Big Impact questions force you to look upstream—to look at the nature of work, customer experience, and company policy. There are a number of different Big Impact questions, and they can vary depending on the organization. But for Eli Lilly and Company, the question was: **Who exactly is our customer?**

It seems simple, right? But most companies never really take the time to approach this question with a beginner's mind, because they already think that they know, so why explore further?

Here's why the Big Impact questions matter: Tactics before strategy is a dangerous recipe. Would you take off without a flight plan? You might be making great time in a super-efficient airplane, and the wind is at your back . . . but you're headed toward the wrong destination.

> **NOTE**
>
> Big Impact questions—like "Who is our customer?—are part of a framework that stands the test of time. Regardless of how the input mechanism changes, or the process, or the technology, Big Impact questions are the first step in looking for new results.

It's what you learn after you know it all that really counts.
                    John Wooden, UCLA Basketball Coach

"We bundled the customer question with two others," Christi explains, as she brushes back her hair. "'Who is the customer' was joined with 'What is the customer's experience? and Why does it matter?'"

When you're in the business of saving lives, sooner or later (one hopes sooner?) somebody is going to ask:

Why are we doing this, and who are we doing it for?

"Everybody could rally around the patient," Christi shares. "So to that 'higher order purpose' and in those 'emotional connections' that people have, employees did not argue that the patient was important. The patient is the reason why we are here."

According to Christi, "Who's the most important customer?" was the sticking point. "It wasn't whether or not the patient mattered," she explained, because everyone knew that the patient was a priority. To answer the customer question, she began with agreement—consensus—around the relevance (and territorial perceptions) within Lilly. "We weren't competing with the relevance of a particular department or customer set."

When they stopped the turf war conversation around "Am I relevant? Do my focus and area matter?" attention could be paid to something else: *How*?

How do we create more relevance, more connection, and more understanding of the customer throughout the organization?

However, in order to reach the patient, Lilly touched many customers. The doctor, for example, prescribed the medication. The hospital pharmacy, or the local pharmacy, stocked the medication. The insurers approved and paid—in part or in full—for the medications. Aren't these important customers? Doesn't selling to a pharmacy or hospital matter more than selling to an individual doctor or (here comes the heresy part) an individual patient?

In a complex value chain, finding the customer wasn't a "slam dunk." And there was one other wrinkle that made Christi's job even more difficult. Much of the company's workforce is made up of healthcare professionals and medical employees. "To them, the word 'customer' could feel slimy. The fact that we are profitable doing what we do seemed counterintuitive to the more philanthropic postures that some like to entertain. So it was a bit of a conflict for some people even to use the word 'customer,' because they were there to provide care."

Here's where some valuable research uncovered an important data point, providing insight for even the most altruistic idealists at Lilly. They worked with a research company that asked thousands of people to "self-describe" as part of the data gathering. When asked to describe their role and their interaction with the company that made their medication, 100 percent of responses described a customer role—not a patient role. No one self-described as a patient. "And this was out of tens of thousands of journals," Christi revealed. "So when we really looked at it, we reached a new understanding.

"We realized that people view themselves as multidimensional, and we all have roles to play—sister, daughter, mother, neighbor, volunteer advocate, leader—whatever you'd like to say. But you were only a patient to your healthcare provider. So we really had to help people see that patients are customers of Lilly because, ultimately, they (the patients) have a choice. They have a choice whether to take the medication. They can choose to pursue a different course of treatment, try another medication, or choose not to take our medicines at all. When we started helping employees to see our business from a patient's perspective, it helped the medical community here to understand that patients are customers."

She continued, "We define the customer as the person who takes our medication—and anyone who enables the customer to achieve an improved outcome. Customers are patients, just not patients of Eli Lilly and Company."

For any industry, here's a useful definition about the customer:

1. The customer is anyone upon whom your success depends.
2. The customer is someone who has a choice of whether or not she does business with you.
3. Anyone who enables an improved outcome in your value chain is your customer.

But don't always assume that finding your customer involves following the money. Because, as we will see in later chapters, *transactions and value are two very different things*. For example, value can also be about ease. If customer experience were only about money, every time I needed to mail something, I would probably go to the U.S. Postal Service. Because money-wise, that's the cheapest. Well, what's my experience like when I go there? If I said that it wasn't so great, would you argue with me? Because we could have that conversation in the line at the post office, and you'd have plenty of time to make your point.

In return for cost savings, I'm exchanging time and suffering, in my experience. Am I willing to do that? That value equation doesn't always work for me. In the B2B space, value comes from relationships, experience, ease of use, and being able to get something back for the money that you're spending. Companies that see the customer beyond the transaction will sell more, find more customers, and can potentially disrupt the marketplace.

Finding the Big Impact customer means looking past just sheer outlay of money, cost savings, or transactions. For big pharma, looking at the big pharmacy (or chain of pharmacies) wasn't necessarily where they found the most value.

Identifying the right customer is vital to your business, no matter what market you serve. So many businesses today are guessing wrong around customer experience. Or they're not even making a guess. These organizations are going full steam ahead with the seven most dangerous words in business:

"That's the way we've always done things."

Big Impact questions point in the direction of change. Or more specifically, progress. And progress like that always requires dominoes.

No, you don't need to order a pizza. I'm talking about the game of dominoes. Let me explain:

One of my favorite things to do is to spend time with my three phenomenal goddaughters (you can say that I'm biased, but I would say that I'm just telling the truth). They are engaging, energetic, and smart young ladies.

Piper, the middle one, is 11. Because she was recently cast in the school musical, *Shrek*, she is currently sporting a shoulder-length bob with green tips in her hair. She made the color change because she had to have her headshots done for the show. Brynn is the baby, but don't call her that. She's nine and has pigtails. Big sis' is Lorelei, the future scientist, who usually supervises any game that we play. And play is what we all love to do. Especially when it comes to the game of dominoes.

These girls have never lost the love of building domino chains. You know this activity, right? You're trying to create a configuration of dominoes so that when you hit the lead one, everything falls into place. Do it right and they hit one another, falling into this beautiful pattern.

The setup leads to this wonderful payoff moment. For these girls, it's pure delight—plus I get a kick out of seeing the smiles on their faces. We all light up when we see what we've set in motion together.

One of the lessons that I've learned from building lots of domino chains with my three amigas is that the more complicated curving and longer the chain, the more challenging it is to create the alignment that's needed.

Lorelei says that one of the most satisfying chains is actually the straight line. "Because what happens is, you quickly set it up," she says with a toss of her hair, keeping an eye on her little sisters as they fiddle with the camera and a small tripod, "You quickly knock it down, but you get to see it working right away." She's big into STEM (science, technology, engineering, and math) programs at her school. So she always wants to know how to make things work—and make them work better.

But picture this scenario: When I'm with my goddaughters and we build a domino chain that has 120 pieces in it, that could take us an hour to set up. So 45 minutes in, if Piper gets up to grab a root beer and she knocks it all down, how do we feel? "That's never good!" Brynn says, as she stops in her tracks. "Hey . . . wait a minute! How did Piper get a root beer?"

The frustration level is incredibly high after the dominoes are unintentionally toppled. It's discouraging to start over when dealing with a long chain. But when we build them with 10 dominoes and somebody accidentally kicks it over on the way to a juice box or whatever, it's no big deal.

Dominoes is a game that works because of energy. To be technical, the kinetic energy and gravitational force is what drives momentum, whether your chain is 10 or 10,000 dominoes long.

When one of the girls loses interest and becomes disengaged, energy literally goes out of the room; it's the same thing when you lose momentum inside your organization.

In fact, disengagement can lead to destruction. The kid who's getting bored/not feeling engaged/not feeling part of the team might even make a mock gesture of knocking over the dominoes. It's an attention-getting move. Ever seen it happen in your company?

Have you ever had an executive sponsor or senior leader emphasize the importance of listening to the customer, only to lose interest before the first domino falls into place? Did someone in the C-Suite kick over your project?

When your stakeholders, executives, and customers no longer feel engaged, they don't feel part of an important process. If that disengagement occurs, your sponsors will literally destroy what they helped to create. And just like sisters who ruin one another's hard work, betrayal from the inside out is difficult to accept. And to overcome.

What people are telling you when they attempt to kick over your dominoes is, "This isn't working for me."

Energy has to be present for dominoes to work. Natural forces propel the dominoes forward, transferring kinetic energy forward until the last domino falls. To keep energy and engagement inside the process, the girls talk about how good things are going to look, how much we will enjoy seeing the video (which is when Brynn grabs my camera phone), how we all find satisfaction in a job well done. Engagement and support are the only ways that we stay on top of things, and a culture of collaboration is the ultimate result.

Keeping people engaged and involved and focused on the prize—whether it's a cool video like this one (https://bit.ly/listenup-playdominoes)—or an innovative insight into what really matters within the company. Both of those results require engagement at every step in the process.

You build something, you watch it unfold, and you are surprised and engaged and smiling and wondering and . . . discovering. And so are your customers.

What would you do if you didn't know for certain who your customer was?

The beginner's mindset tackles questions from an unexpected place— a powerful, eye-opening place that is counterintuitive. A place that challenges your expertise and well-thought-out beliefs. That place is described in three words:

I don't know.

Could you or your team start there, too?

Christi's challenge was helping the highly educated and extremely talented team at Lilly to look at what they didn't know.

For the team at Lilly, that wasn't easy. Because they knew a lot. Fortunately, the scientific approach to their market worked to Christi's advantage.

Scientists understand that every outcome around an experiment is a good outcome. If you don't prove your hypothesis, that result informs your next one. Every experiment has value, and testing a hypothesis isn't about proving yourself right. Informing your next move is the outcome that matters. That's true only 100 percent of the time. Because it's science, my friend, science. That's how things work.

Christi found her first domino inside of Lilly. She knew that she needed executive support, especially as she was making people uncomfortable by calling patients "customers." New ideas can be hard to contemplate without guidance from the C-Suite.

Because of her 26-year tenure at the company, Christi understood the source of kinetic energy inside of Lilly—the company's corporate policies, called "The Red Book" (https://bit.ly/listenup-redbook). This manifesto of values, developed over time since the days following the Civil War, puts passion into action. "People all over the world are counting on us," the Red Book says.

By acknowledging the company's values, Christi made her business case around customer experience from a position of collaboration—alignment—leveraging that higher sense of purpose so that executive sponsors and frontline employees could see that redefining the customer was the most caring thing they could do.

"We're still the only pharma company that takes an enterprise lens on this (issue of the customer value chain). And you can look at our performance, and it's going well, a lot of things are there that some people attribute to our overall customer centricity," Christi says.

But has it been a success?

"I can't . . . I still don't know that I would call it a success," she says candidly, as she looks out of the conference room window. She realizes that this kind of strategic work is never really finished. You can never stop asking the Big Impact questions—not if you care about your customers.

"I think the biggest thing is really recognizing what problem you are trying to solve. And so, in starting there, it allows you to know if customer experience (CX) is really at the heart of your problem. And CX probably is, but until people can understand the fact that we have a customer experience problem, there's not a lot of interest in customer experience improvement." Connection is the key. "Making sure that there is a clear customer experience element to the problem that you're trying to solve—because there almost always is. That's what people can recognize. It helps everyone to find that commitment by connecting those things."

What would it mean to you if your entire team had the same definition of who your customer is? What if you connected the values of your company to the values of your customer?

Maybe you're not in the business of saving lives. But your customers are the source of your livelihood, no matter where you work, even if you literally work at Dominoes®.

Find that Big Impact customer. Share data with your executive sponsors so that your initiatives are only the most logical alternative. (We'll talk more about how to do that in future chapters.) But for now, just remember:

A simple game can have profound implications.

Finding the right customer is finding the best and first domino—the one that's going to create the right motion within your value chain.

CHAPTER 5

When Organizations Are Out of Alignment

I called in a favor. Now I was on the hot seat.

I had asked an executive sponsor to help me out by coordinating a mandatory meeting of the senior staff. There was an issue with the company's customer experience strategy. Something wasn't working, and I needed the entire team to discover how to fix it. I reminded my sponsor that customer experience was the prime directive for the year ahead. He nodded his head in agreement. "It's done. I'll get you the meeting," he said.

That day, inside the executive conference room, the natives were restless. By "natives," I mean the vice presidents and division leaders across the entire organization. My sponsor was sitting in the first row with his arms crossed, watching people tap on their phones and sip coffee.

The tilt of his head was saying, "Where are we going to go today, Karen?" The lack of a smile was saying, "This better be good."

He stood up and turned to face the room. "Thank you for coming, everyone," he said, giving me the side eye. "Please take your seats and wrap up whatever messages you are sending. Karen is ready to begin."

Better get right to the point, I thought to myself.

"I'm willing to cancel today's meeting," I began. Everyone stopped looking at their phones. All eyes were on me now. "If you will only complete one simple task." The senior leaders contemplated my offer.

"Please pick up the sticky notepad that is on the table in front of each of you. All I need you to do is to write down your answer to this question: 'What is our customer experience strategy?' I'll then ask you to stick your note on the board. Once we see the common themes are in complete alignment, I can give you your day back."

The entire room grinned. The participants looked at each other. Then they glanced at the stickies on the table. In unison these senior leaders picked up the nearby pens. Hoping this meeting would end as quickly as it began, the team started on the easiest exercise since God invented jumping jacks.

Eventually, all of the pens were replaced. One by one, the leaders walked quickly and confidently toward the board. Without fanfare, the Post-its® were stuck on the board.

That's when the fights broke out.

No two executives had the same definition of the customer experience strategy! I didn't even have to prompt them to look at the messages. They were already looking. From what I could see, things didn't look too good.

Even though this strategy was the company's top mission—their number-one priority for the year ahead—confusion ruled the room.

Instantly, there was a bouillabaisse of bickering: "Wait just a minute!" one exec said, kneeling to frown at one of the notes. "That's just wrong!" His colleague interrupted him, pointing at her note: "You're not seeing what really matters here!" and a third joined in the middle with a "Surely you can't be serious? Our largest customer is the only one that matters?! Yeah, right!"

Voices toppled over voices. No one could finish a sentence. The conversation escalated in volume, passion, and finger-pointing.

Now it was my turn for a little side eye of my own. I shot a quick glance at my executive sponsor.

He shrugged his shoulders. "You're right," he said, standing up. "Stop, everybody, stop!" He was almost shouting at the group. He lowered his voice, "We've got some work to do."

What about you and your team—is there a cohesive and consistent understanding of your customer experience strategy? Do you have some work to do?

I've said it before: Simple questions can have profound answers, because they often point at the nature of how things work and highlight the underlying assumptions that need to change.

C-Sparks: Test Your Alignment

Why wait to try this exercise? Here's what you need:

- Sticky notes
- Sharpies

- Sponsor(s)
- Beginner's mindset: a willingness to discover new things

Bring your leadership team together and ask them to write down their answers to: "What is our customer experience strategy?"

For extra credit, try this one: "What customer problem is our digital transformation strategy going to solve—or try to solve?" (more on "Defining the Digital Divide" in the next chapter).

But wait just a minute. Does this exercise smell like a hunt for a mission statement? If you're hoping to find alignment and unity around a policy, remember how mission statements work:

If 10 people say the same words in 10 different situations to 10 different audiences, do those words have the same meaning? No—making a mission statement into a mantra involves memorization, not meaning. Saying certain words isn't the same as delivering the meaning behind the words.

Mission statements and strategic visions are important, but to quote my ninth-favorite Eighties band, Extreme, "more than words" is what matters, when it comes to customer feedback.

ACTION IS WHERE MANTRAS AND MISSIONS COME TO LIFE

Exactly what kind of experience are customers wanting from companies? In a 2019 survey completed by Salesforce (https://bit.ly/listenup-salesforcesurvey -2019) featuring input from over 23,000 respondents, 84 percent of consumers said that the experience a company provides is as important as its products and services. For business buyers, that number jumps to 89 percent. That's an 8 percent increase from 2018 (https://www.salesforce.com/blog/2018/06 /digital-customers-research.html), and the trend is only going to continue, because the line between products and services is blurred, but the customer experience is crystal clear.

Think about going in to buy a car. Perhaps you are fortunate enough to purchase a Lexus. That automobile is a beautiful product. But unless you have $56,423 in your wallet right now, you are going to need financing. So you need a service (finance) in order to buy the product (the car). And when you bring it in for an oil change, there are certainly products involved in that transaction (the oil filter, for example), but an oil change is a service. So is owning a Lexus a product or a service?

The modern answer is neither. The reason that people buy a Lexus isn't because of the kind of oil filters offered, or financing, or even the navigation and horsepower inside the vehicle. Because all of those aspects, combined with the people who deliver them, create the truly unique aspect of the brand. Customers buy a Lexus because of the *experience.*

Steve Cannon (https://bit.ly/listenup-SteveCannon), President and CEO of Mercedes Benz USA says, "Customer experience better be at the top of your list when it comes to priorities in your organization." He continues his truth tale, "Customer experience is the new marketing."

Shifting out of the familiar realm of consumer purchases in the B2B space, 82 percent of business buyers say that just one extraordinary experience raises their expectations of other companies. What if you could find and sustain that level of extraordinary experience?

Maybe you're still afraid to ask your customers the ultimate relationship question: *"Do these scores make me look fat?"*

That's a tough question in any relationship, because it asks for the ultimate tradeoff decision: Honesty or flattery? Hope or reality?

What message do you want to hear from your customer?

How often does your customer feedback tell you what you want to hear rather than what you need to know?

You may have experienced the "I NEED A FIVE!" epidemic. You take your car in for service, and the technician asks you to complete a survey, adding, "I would really appreciate a score of five on every question."

An appliance is delivered to your home. The delivery person asks you to complete a quick survey, and adds, "I'll get my bonus if you give me all fives."

You comply. Bonuses are paid. Employees are rewarded. Executives congratulate themselves on achieving a high level of customer loyalty. But being pressured into a generous five doesn't mean I'm being totally honest, now does it? Passing out fives costs me nothing. But if there's more to the story than just a score, that five could be costing you in customer loyalty.

If you consistently achieve your customer experience improvement targets, are you measuring what matters to your customers?

Perfect scores may indicate what's working, what behaviors to continue, and what processes have improved. And those scores make us feel good about our own performance. But it's a false sense of security, because I'm here to tell you what only a good friend will: Those scores make you look fat.

Do perfect scores alert you to risks? Competitive threats? When a customer is about to leave you? New engagements or sales opportunities?

C-Sparks: Challenge the Scoreboard

If your customer metrics are more frequently cause for celebration than for concern:

Don't Stop at the Score: Review Customer Comments! Do your customer survey scores mirror your customer comments? A customer may give you a perfect score—congratulations! Please don't stop there. Look at the comments and the narrative to really find the gold. Then provide three suggestions for improvement. Written comments provide clues about new questions to ask and new experiences to measure.

Share More to Score. Share your metrics with your customer and ask what's missing from his or her POV (point of view). Your business is changing, but are you changing your metrics of customer success? Are you measuring your customer's world as it exists today (with your business process changes reflected in your questions)? Sharing your metrics is a great place to start discovering *relevance*. Don't stop with what your team thinks is most important—get the customer to confirm your suspicions. Is what you're measuring aligned with where your customers are now and the experience you want to deliver?

Match customer feedback scores with customer purchase behaviors. Do highly satisfied customers make future purchases? How frequently? Look for customers who tell you that they like you and then spend like they don't. Contact those customers to understand why their purchasing patterns have changed. Find what's missing—close the gap between intention and action.

Review your recognition and rewards programs. Are you buying high satisfaction and loyalty scores? The best incentives are provided for behavior, not grades. Reward action rather than scores. For example, tie compensation to taking action on customer feedback rather than achieving a perfect score. A survey may say "all fives," but reward the employee who calls to follow up based on comments, or one who just goes the extra mile. The score is never the whole story!

It's one thing to say, "I have a vision," but it's another thing entirely to create alignment around that vision. You have to get back to the customer view: their hiring policies, objectives, processes, what they measure . . . and ultimately what you deliver.

The message isn't the mission. The customer is.

If you want to create alignment, don't stop with memorized words. Look at the actions that people are taking to connect with the customer. And then comes the ultimate test: What did the customer do differently as a result?

Our greatest obligation is not to confuse slogans with solutions.
Walter Winchell, American Journalist and Reporter

Do you enjoy watching sports with your family? When I was growing up, basketball tickets at the local university were the hottest tickets in town. In fact, those tickets were appreciating in value as the season went on—and it had nothing to do with the team's won/lost record. The university did something that kept season ticket holders hungry for more—literally.

To encourage fans to stay for the entire basketball game, the university launched a new promotion. If the home team held their opponents to 49 points or less, each fan won a free fried chicken dinner at a local restaurant. Thus, every person in that stadium was watching the scoreboard with a new level of engagement.

I'll never forget the first blowout game—I could almost smell free fried chicken, and so could 6,000 of my hungriest basketball-loving friends. With three minutes remaining in the game, the opposing team had just 40 points on the board. The home team was in the lead by a commanding margin. Yet, the stadium was still full—pulsing with excitement.

With one minute left in the game, fans were on their feet. Clapping! Screaming! Chanting . . .

"Chicken! CHICKEN! CHICK-EN!!!!!!!"

With 15 seconds left in the game, the announcers could not be heard above the deafening crowd. The ravenous appetite for free fried meat could not be denied.

Was this free fried chicken dinner being served at an elite restaurant? *No.*

Was it an expensive dinner? *No.* The approximate cost was $4.25, complete with side dishes and drink.

Then why did the campaign work? Because defense is delicious? *No.*

It worked for one reason: **There's a difference between being interested and being invested.**

If fans were merely interested in the final score of the game, they could have easily read it the next morning. They could have beaten the traffic by leaving the game early. They could have had a head start on celebrating a home team victory.

That free chicken dinner converted interest into investment. Suddenly, each person in the stadium owned a piece of the success. Each person had something of tangible value to gain.

How often are you interested in your customers' feedback, rather than invested?

You launch surveys. You host listening tours. You hold focus groups. Your internal stakeholders avalanche you with customer research requests.

You complete the research. You present it. What happens next? Does someone take action? Does change occur? Or is the leadership audience bored by a blowout? "Our scores are good, I'm going home at halftime."

Excellent teams, like excellent organizations, play full out for the entire game.

C-Sparks: Are you interested or invested?

The NEW ROI: Return on Insights. Identify the places where customer feedback translates into actions—and measurable results. Are your customers interested or invested in taking action around their feedback?

> **Charge for your services.** When your stakeholders invest time, money, and headcount in a customer research project, they move from the sidelines to the arena. Shared costs quickly indicate where this project sits on the list of priorities.
>
> **Create a "to do" list with owners.** When customers identify problems to be solved, someone must be accountable to fix the problem. When you see your name next to an action item, you're more likely to do it than to volunteer on your own.
>
> **Recognize and reward success.** Similar to the free fried chicken dinner, the reward does not need to be expensive. It's a tool for incenting your stakeholders to invest in customer success.

My friends in Mexico City shared a saying with me: *Entre dicho y hecho hay mucho trecho.* Literally, there's a lot of distance between saying and doing. And figuratively, "It's easier said than done." Sitting on the sidelines and playing the blame game is easier than creating alignment.

Saying that you are customer focused and running a customer-centric business is truly a question of culture and commitment.

In the coming chapters, we're going to talk more about how to get your organization on board, creating engagement from executives and every facet of your company. But for now, when it comes to alignment, some top priorities and payoffs need to be highlighted. More importantly, there's a new understanding around what exactly is at stake. As businesses become more and more commoditized, the battle for differentiation becomes incredibly fierce.

Being competitive—and playing to win—mean looking at what matters most, so that you can approach your customers with an informed perspective and the understanding that the rules of customer engagement have changed. As a result, the old playbook is out of date.

Research from Salesforce (https://bit.ly/listenup-salesforcesurvey-2018) in a 2019 study with over 23,000 responses shows that the top priorities for modern marketers are as follows:

- Engage with customers in real time.
- Optimize the marketing mix for best return (ROI).
- Modernize tools and techniques.
- Create a shared, single view of customers across business units.
- Unify customer data sources.

Delivering on these five key areas requires a shift in the marketing mix. Customer alignment doesn't just rely on the "Four P's": product, price, promotion, and place. The aligned organization focuses on the fifth P: *personalization*.

> Get closer than ever to your customers. So close that you tell them
> what they need well before they realize it themselves.
>
> *Steve Jobs*

For retail customers, 91 percent prefer brands that provide personalized offers and recommendations; 74 percent of these consumers will actively share data in exchange for personalized experiences. At the center of this exchange is trust. And what technological tools can help build that trust?

For the B2B companies with whom I work, expanding wallet share is always a priority. Companies want to have a more holistic conversation with customers so that they are offering and recommending new solutions.

Online or in person, expanding the conversation leads to new opportunities. After all, if it happens online when consumers are buying children's toys, golf clubs, and coffee makers, why can't it happen when businesses connect?

Perhaps it's because of the sheer amount of data out there. According to *Forbes* (https://bit.ly/listenup-Forbes1), there are 6,000 tweets posted on Twitter every second. In that same second, 4,400 calls are started on Skype and 972 images are uploaded to Instagram. As I write those numbers, I wonder what they will be by the time you're reading these words? The point is that there's a lot of noise out there. A lot of queries for connection. Voices wanting to be heard. Customers who need what your company can provide. Are you listening, and are you personalizing your response?

It's not surprising that in a survey of 350 global marketing leaders, nearly 80 percent felt only partially prepared to deliver the localized and personalized experiences desired by customers. Forrester (https://bit.ly/listenup -Forrester1) says that 89 percent of digital businesses—including companies like Coca-Cola, Netflix, Sephora, and Wells Fargo—are investing in personalization.

The top five benefits of personalization include the following:

- Increased visitor engagement
- Improved customer experience
- Improved brand perception
- Increased conversion rates
- Increased lead generation and customer acquisition

It's time to go from said to done, aligning your organization around the biggest payoffs in customer satisfaction, connection, and engagement. Leading companies aren't afraid to leverage new technology and training to get there. In the next chapter, we'll see how digitalization and personalization are combining for best-of-breed companies, and how new tech tools are delivering one-to-one connections in surprising ways.

CHAPTER 6

Defining the Digital Divide

My mistake was showing up on time.

My friends were excited to show off their newly remodeled home. Walking up the driveway, I saw the beautiful candles in the windows, the manicured lawn—a truly gorgeous setting. I rang the doorbell with my right hand, holding the bottle of wine in my left.

When the door opened, I was greeted with an odd sensation. My friends, the husband an MD and the wife a PhD, were trying hard to be happy to see me, but they couldn't quite get there. I had the feeling that I had just walked in on a couple having an argument. I discovered my intuition was right.

They invited me in, trying to make the best of whatever it was I had walked into. I've been there: hosting an event, running behind schedule, and trying to smile pretty for the guests. But something was wrong with this picture.

As I scanned the room, the renovations were impressive. Elegant. Comfortable. But when I saw the picture window, I paused. What was that?

A stepladder, partially hung drapes, and an array of discarded tools were strewn about in a makeshift heap. It looked like the toolbox had thrown up after having duct tape for breakfast. Ah, perhaps this unfortunate pile was the source of the tension?

These smart and charming people had all the right gear for hanging drapes and blinds. As the evening unfolded, they relaxed enough to share a candid story: they didn't really know how to use their tools. They had everything they needed but couldn't get what they wanted—and their first guest had just rung their doorbell!

The pressure of trying to deliver time-bound results (especially for prompt guests, like me) doesn't help. Being smart isn't the same as having deep expertise, especially when it comes to making your beautiful home into exactly what you want. Overcoming a lack of understanding was compounded by the drive to get results. It turns out that this remodel left more than just the living room window exposed.

The tension between my friends reminded me of the tension I've seen in the executive office, time and time again. Pressure to perform leads companies to invest in tools—you might even say a standard toolkit of digital data gathering, customer insights, and more. Tools that, on the surface, you might say, "Everyone knows how to use them." But is that really true?

If I put a paintbrush in your hand, you certainly understand the concept of paint and the tools involved in putting color on a wall—or on a piece of canvas. But that doesn't make you Picasso. In fact, it doesn't even mean that you can repaint your bathroom without getting weird marks on the ceiling (take a look, I think you missed a spot).

After the initial tension subsided (there had been a heated conversation about those tools just before I arrived as they were trying to figure out what to do with them), we chatted about some of their challenges. Here's what we discovered:

A hammer can help you to create a home—or destroy it.

When a hammer hits a nail head on, it creates force to break through barriers like walls, for example. But when that same hammer misses the mark, it leads to destruction. Glaring holes. Damage. Places that need patching. Drapes that hang at a weird angle.

My friends weren't going to use those standard tools if they couldn't reach a higher standard in their home. They wanted decor, not destruction. Here's what they realized:

Having the right tools is not the same as knowing how to use them.

If they didn't know how to use the tools, they didn't have the right tools for the job.

The same is true for companies. When I ask the clients I meet with on a regular basis about what's top of mind for enabling their customer experience transformation, they often turn to their toolkit, more often than not, the seemingly standard digital transformation toolkit, because there's a pervasive belief that everybody knows how to use digital tools to deliver outstanding customer experiences. Nothing could be further from the truth. As I discovered at that dinner party, a toolkit can sometimes produce tension, complication, and unintended consequences—especially if you don't really know how to use it.

In theory, there is no difference between theory and practice. But in practice, there is.
Yogi Berra, Manager of the NY Yankees and 18-Time Baseball All Star

To extend that idea into the digital realm, digital tools are only as good as the people who program them. Consider these eye-opening results from the 2019–2020 Annual CIO Survey, conducted by Logicalis (https://www.logicalis-thinkhub.com/):

- Forty-one percent of respondents have implemented Artificial Intelligence (AI) in some way. That's double the number from their 2018 survey.
- Despite this increase in adoption, only one in ten respondents (9 percent) believe that their organization has been successful in reaping the rewards of AI technology to enhance customer service.
- Forty-four percent of respondents believe that their organization is not very successful at all when it comes to AI. For instance, almost half of respondents (47 percent) say that existing AI deployments are seeing very little success in marketing and sales, along with 46 percent in finance and operations, 44 percent in customer service, and 42 percent in product service and information

Today, technology is a tool to bring the voice of the customer to your team —and your C-Suite—at the touch of a button. But have you ever found yourself—or your company—trusting too much in tools, instead of listening to the voice of the customer?

YOU ARE NOT ALONE

Having confidence and clarity around tools is really the key to using them effectively. Whatever those tools become in the future—I'm talking about digitalization, AI, and more—the human element is the one that really demands our focus. If we're going to define the digital divide, that conversation doesn't begin with technology. It begins with people.

There's a misunderstanding at work in the marketplace, and you've probably heard it before: digital transformation is the solution. The reality is that digital transformation is only a tool.

As I asked in the previous chapter, What customer problem is your digital transformation trying to solve? The operative word in that sentence isn't "digital." It's "customer." I'm not saying that digital transformation isn't important—it's a trend that's here to stay, and digitalization is only going to become more pervasive. That's why there's never been a greater need for understanding around how to use this tool, so that we never lose sight of the humans—the customers—these tools are built to serve.

> The most dangerous place to make decisions is in the office. You need to make decisions where the customer is.
> *Ulrik Nehammer, Former CEO of Coca-Cola Germany, in* Trailblazer

The stats and chatbots are all built around a very real and human interaction. Just as you wouldn't hire an "Excel Accountant" or "Twitter CMO," focusing on tools and clearly defined processes is putting the cart before the horse. Too much emphasis on the tools means not enough emphasis on the big picture—the people those tools are meant to help.

PEOPLE BEFORE PROCESS

Amsterdam (https://amsterdam.org/en/facts-and-figures.php) is one of my favorite cities in the world. The city is home to 165 canals, eight windmills, 207 Van Gogh paintings, 8,863 buildings built before the 18th century, and one royal palace. A compact 135 square miles (about the size of Philadelphia), this beautiful and historic place is caught between history and expansion, bound by waterways and narrow streets. The city has balanced its Sin City reputation in a context of breathtaking historical buildings and undeniable charm. However, overcrowding and bad behavior have created an environment that's at best inefficient and, at worst, unsafe.

At least, that's what Bert Nap told NPR (https://bit.ly/listenup-amsterdam). Nap lives with his wife and daughter in a cute house beside a chapel that borders a picturesque canal, right in the middle of the Red Light district. He says that he sent his daughter to kindergarten next door to the brothels.

"She grew up waving to the working girls on the way to school," he explains. An author of language textbooks, Nap says he's lived in the same house for 40 years, ever since moving to Amsterdam as a student. He and his wife have been very happy in the city. That is, until Elvis showed up on his doorstep.

Early one morning, Nap was awakened by "a ruckus." On his front porch, he saw the King of Rock and Roll. And Elvis was not alone.

The shouting that woke Nap and his family was provided by a gaggle of Englishmen, all of them dressed as Elvis, hollering right in front of his house. "Why don't you do that in your hometown?" Nap asked the costumed clan. The shortest Elvis with the sideways wig shouted back: "We buy your streets, we are paying for it! Why don't you go live somewhere else?"

Before you think that Elvis makes a good point, don't be cruel. Perhaps suspicious minds would question Nap's decision to live in the middle of that famous district with a daughter. Can you really say that it's now or never for him to leave—when this has been his home for 40 years? While Nap was all shook up, remember that people have been living in this area for centuries—long before the King sang his first solo.

The beauty of Amsterdam is that it's not just for tourists; it's one of the least-expensive capitals in Europe. Combined with the tolerance for which the Netherlands is famous, it's understandable that Nap and his neighbors don't want to move. Bottom line: It's their home!

In 2019, the "I Live Here" campaign (https://bit.ly/listenup-ilivehere) was launched on the heels of 2018's summer message of "Enjoy and Respect." The campaigns featured billboards reminding visitors to treat the city as they would their own. "Amsterdam is first and foremost a city in which people live, and only secondly a tourist destination," says Vera Al, spokeswoman for Amsterdam's deputy mayor.

But the city council had to answer a nagging question: How can residents and tourists coexist in safety and harmony?

HOW BIG IS TOURISM IN AMSTERDAM?

Amsterdam allows for behavior that would get people thrown in jail in other cities, which is part of its appeal. The freedoms afforded to tourists have created a bit of a prison for its residents and safety concerns for the municipality.

Over the last 10 years (https://bit.ly/listenup-amsterdamstats), tourism has more than doubled in Amsterdam. Local authorities say that revenues from tourism amount to well over 10.3 billion Euros ($11.3 billion USD). For 2020, it's estimated that nearly 20 million people will visit the city. Mayor Femke Halsema expects 29 million in 2025, according to DW.com (https://bit.ly/listenup-ilivehere). CNN projections (https://bit.ly/listenup-visitors) show 42 million expected visitors in 2030, or more than 50 times the current population!

Compare the current number of annual Amsterdam visitors (about 20 million) to the following cities and sites:

Berlin: 13.5 million

Hawaii: 9.3 million

The Louvre Museum in Paris: 8.5 million

The Colosseum in Rome: 6.9 million

The Eiffel Tower: 6.7 million
Versailles: 5.9 million

Source: Travel and Leisure Magazine (https://bit.ly/listenup-destinations)

TRANSPORTATION CONSIDERATIONS

The city's Schiphol Airport is bursting under the burden of popularity as well, according to Airporttechnology.com (https://bit.ly/listenup-aero). In 2018, Amsterdam's airport had a limit of 500,000 flight movements a year. (They actually tracked exactly 499,446 landings and takeoffs—that's cutting it close!) Servicing approximately 71 million passengers now, a new three-story pier and terminal expansion was scheduled for completion in late 2020. The new additions will increase capacity by about 14 million passengers.

In an effort to curb overtourism, in 2016 the city implemented a "hotel stop," which is a ban on new properties. According to *Vastgoed* journal (https://bit.ly/listenup-vastgoed), there are currently 516 hotels in Amsterdam, totaling 36,834 rooms. Even with the hotel stop from the pandemic, 8,133 rooms are in the process of being added (thanks to construction permits already in the pipeline before the ban took effect). Net result? There will be a 22 percent increase in hotel rooms in the very near future.

REDEFINING CROWDSOURCING

While we have some data on where future tourists might sleep, where will they go when they are awake? Crowded and narrow city streets explode during popular events, such as football games at the local arena. Foot traffic is a huge concern for city officials, police officers, and business owners. The ability to move around safely and easily impacts the customer experience directly: being trapped in a crowd on a narrow street isn't pleasant, and depending on who's coming up behind you, it might not be very safe.

Heralded as one of the most bike-friendly cities in the world, a drunken or stoned tourist pedaling through Amsterdam at rush hour won't make many friends. In fact, the combination of freedom and bike wheels (https://bit.ly /listenup-Amsterdamlife) can be a playbook for disaster. With 900,000 bicycles in the municipality, there's a lot of pedestrian traffic that needs to be managed and policed. Beyond airports and hotels, the city's people-moving systems (buses, trains, and ferries, for example) are impacted by the movement of humans and bicycles. Law enforcement officers have to be aware of where the crowds are and where they aren't for safety considerations. Amsterdam wants people to have fun but stay safe doing it, so the City Council needed a way to anticipate and mitigate impending risks. From crowd control to wayfinding, how could they enhance the experience of both tourists and residents, providing an environment that was not only safe, but efficient?

Experience management matters in Amsterdam. From city to citizen and city to guest, the local authorities sought ways to gather data that would be informative, but not intrusive. How would you go about gathering the information that would matter most, when the customer just happens to be millions of residents and tourists?

There wasn't a realistic opportunity to survey nearly 20 million people, but the city's leadership didn't have to. The City of Amsterdam hired Royal HaskoningDHV to engineer a safer and more efficient city. How did they do it?

Eelco Thiellier (https://wi.st/2YHnjEO) is the lead engineer for Royal Haskoning's City of Amsterdam project. For his team, the challenge was crowd management, movement, and safety: measuring and predicting crowds would improve everyone's experience, from police officers to partiers, residents, and visiting football fans. Thiellier used a combination of Wi-Fi data and strategically placed cameras to develop predictive algorithms of where people were congregating. It was like a yield management exercise for big events, businesses, and people movement within the city.

But before you can say, "Big Brother," Thiellier explains that their methodology maintains privacy. "No personal data was used at any point," he shares, acknowledging the importance of privacy, stakeholder management, and customer experience. As you might expect, the residents and visitors to Amsterdam value their confidentiality.

Privacy informed the way that the team gathered their data. This trend is echoed elsewhere. In an AMA survey commissioned by Duke University (https://bit.ly/listenup-CMOSurvey), marketers anticipate a 40.2 percent increase in trusting relationships as part of the value equation. Gathering data with respect to privacy is at the center of any well-thought-out digital strategy, and the Amsterdam team couldn't afford to violate that trust.

A SINGLE SIGNAL IS EFFECTIVELY FALSE

A system of video cameras was united with Wi-Fi tracking as part of a MaaS solution (mobility as a service). "We use Wi-Fi to track the device, not the person," he explains. They didn't need to know who had what phone, just that there were a certain number of devices moving through a particular area. "We just needed to sniff them," he says, referring to gathering aggregate data on the number of devices in a specific zone.

That intelligence was combined with information from standard street cameras and sensors that the team placed throughout the city. Because a single signal is effectively false, knowing that a crowd has gathered isn't the same as understanding why—or devising a solution to address the congestion. Deeper investigation, using a combination of signals and multiple sources, was critical to the team's work. Just as you can't use a single score like NPS to decide everything you do, you've got to have diverse inputs to compose a more useful solution.

Using prevalent common algorithms, the team at Royal Haskoning-DHV was able to determine whether an object was a person, a bicycle, or an umbrella, for example. "We even have the ability to identify a sausage," he says, without a hint of irony. "Perhaps one day we will be able to identify a weapon, such as a gun or a knife."

Using overhead cameras that track the movement of crowds, Thiellier describes how this work impacts the arrivals and departures of trains, ferries, and other public transportation. With detailed information about the movement of people at a particular time of day, resources (such as trains to Belgium, or ferries to the north side of town) can be better allocated. More importantly, design considerations can be applied to the layout and track selection for train stations. City planners can predict how many ferries they need on a Thursday afternoon, or a Friday night, in a particular section of the city.

Safety, accessibility, and comfort were the three main KPIs (key performance indicators) for the project. Traditional systems were already in place for automobile traffic; the team concentrated on pedestrian traffic and two-wheeled pedaled vehicles. "We wanted to make movement within Amsterdam seamless, easy, and pleasurable," Thiellier explains.

Daniel van Motman is the program manager for the new tools. "The crowd-monitoring system gives us insight into the number of pedestrians, mainly near tourist attractions. Where is it in danger of overcrowding?" he asks, rhetorically. Because that answer can now be provided for crowd managers as well as police.

"As a policeman, it will mainly help me to prevent calamities caused by too many people in a small area," says Misha Nauman, a local officer. "If we know where problems will arise, we can take preventative measures." As a result, police actions in Amsterdam can be proactive instead of reactive.

A signal appears on a dashboard in the police station, showing a certain number of people located in a specific area "not as individuals, but as a mass," Nauman points out. "We can tell where it is exactly and how to solve for (any potential danger)" by guiding people toward less crowded areas. Motman agrees—the "crowdedness" at peak times is what makes people uncomfortable.

"As an engineer, I would be happy just placing a sensor and monitoring the masses," Thiellier affirms, recognizing his personal affinity for technology. "But what kind of problem are you solving when you put that sensor there? The great thing about this project is that the enduser and the technology really come together." From the police to the promoters at the arena (and other entrepreneurs in the Red Light District), the crowd experience has improved.

> What people think of as the moment of discovery is really the discovery of the question.
>
> *Jonas Salk, Creator of the Polio Vaccine*

"Before we try to solve the problem, we need to truly understand the problem," Thiellier confirms. For a particular area, such as the Red Light District, the team asked how many people are using it now? What street(s) are experiencing heavy traffic? Is there a slowdown due to an altercation, a parade, a shortage of ferries, a particularly popular "window display," or what exactly? Can we offer rerouting information, or could officials redirect people toward streets or alleyways because of overcongestion? What's the impact on the train station—Is it empty, or busy, at a given time of night? These questions and more were addressed using a combination of digital data.

But the team also employed what Thiellier calls "sweet measures," interviewing individuals to find out what their experience was like and using those stories to reconfirm the details in the data. Simply closing off certain areas wasn't the answer—the city leaders demanded freedom of movement. Instead of suggesting barriers, the team focused on the human element and how to find greater mobility, not less.

Three major areas were impacted for the City of Amsterdam: People, Environment, and Means of Transport. Armed with information around pedestrian movement, the city leaders were better able to predict the following:

- How many ferries to put in the waterways to move people on any given day
- How many ferries they would need to order each season (the ordering process takes time, and being able to plan for future purchases was a plus for the city)
- How to route and reroute bike and pedestrian traffic
- How to detect potential safety risks and alert authorities on how to intervene proactively

The bottom line was reduced crime, reduced patrols, increased tourism, and increased capacity (even within already constrained resources). Less waiting, less congestion, and more available transportation means greater accessibility.

And for the businesses in town, greater potential for profitability, improved safety, and an enhanced experience for their customers (courtesy of the city).

The tools that the team employed included video cameras, sophisticated algorithms, Wi-Fi data, and more.

- Strategically, they looked closely at the problem that they were trying to solve: How would our digital strategy impact the human experience within the city?
- Tactically, they conducted hotspot analysis and corroborated details on cameras in order to gain a complete picture of overcrowded locations.
- Operationally, they showed their unique ways of "listening" translated data into action: their real-time monitoring impacted police presence and provided better pedestrian routing on streets as well as waterways.

The ultimate result? Happier residents and visitors. Data informed the people who use it, including the "customers" of the city. The digital tools will impact the experience of everyone who happens to be within the city limits, balancing privacy with possibilities. While Amsterdam continues to wrestle with its future, the city faces its undeniable expansion and popularity with these new tools. What the experience will be like for tourists and residents in the years to come is still unknown. But the city leaders have put tools in place to be better informed—and prepared—for bringing that future to life.

Everyone from Anaheim to Adelaide talks about predictive analytics—using data to see the future and take proactive action. Amsterdam didn't wait for the survey: the city took action in real time, with real results. The city leaders discovered that asking questions about past experience is the slowest boat on the river, if you want to reach a destination that's satisfying to your customers (or residents, as the case may be). Preparing for the future means moving in real time, and that's what Amsterdam realized, collectively, through this journey. The time required to analyze surveys, questions, and data points can slow down results. The actions in Amsterdam show us that predictive listening is still listening, especially when you can proactively anticipate and deliver exceptional experiences without even having to ask.

C-Sparks: Make It Easier for Your Customers to Get Around

- **DoubleDown on Digitalization.** Before you start placing monitors and systems all around your business, remember the real reason why technology even exists—to solve real business problems; that is, what's the problem we're trying to solve here? Because if it's just to satisfy one department's love of a particular tech tool, don't hang that camera until you've really looked at the tangible human impact of digitalization. Double down on your signals—don't just trust one number or one source. Where can you find details that corroborate?

- **Define the Data.** What, in aggregate, shows the customer behavior that you want to encourage? What are the obstacles in your business that don't make it easy to get from Point A to Point B? Do you have a bottleneck on your website, or a disconnect in customer service? Tools serve those who use them, and the best tools are the ones that solve clearly articulated problems. Not sure if you're chasing the right issues? Ask your customer! That way, your investment in tech (and the people who use it) is aligned with the customers you serve.
- **Get Clear on KPIs.** What does success look like? Just as Amsterdam identified three areas of influence (safety, accessibility, and comfort), you must define the areas of influence for your company—and your customers. Of course, we all want delighted customers: define the elements of that delight, work on them, and measure your success as you pursue the goals that matter most to your clients. If you're determining your KPIs without customer input, you're missing a huge opportunity and serving your own agenda instead of the one that matters most. What elements of your new initiatives for expansion matter most to the people using your products? Cocreate your KPIs and you stand a much better chance of delivering what really matters!
- **Expand Your Airport.** If you are operating at or near capacity in a particular department, region, or hub, don't wait and wonder whether you need to invest in additional resources. The data will show you where growth is needed. Often, helping certain areas, teams, or individuals to go from good to great is the smartest investment that you can make. Take a look and see whether the data and traffic support your expansion, because the customer will find the easiest path to do business. If that's not a path to your front door, you have to wonder why! Make a list of the three to five areas where additional capacity or expansion could make a meaningful difference in your business. What's stopping you from expanding your traffic?
- **Trust but Verify.** If you find surprising statistics around a point of entry, get curious. Confirm your suspicions or verify your assumptions with "sweet measures"—talk to the names inside the numbers. Don't stop with data alone; conversations can provide unseen collaboration and opportunity, as we'll see in the next chapter!

CHAPTER 7

Better Questions, Better Answers

I discover more on Sunday afternoons than on any other day of the week. How is that possible?

Well, on Sunday afternoons I spend time with one of the most intellectually curious mentors and teachers I've ever met: my 96-year-old grandfather.

My grandfather is a first-generation American who served in both the Atlantic and Pacific theaters in World War II. He enrolled himself in computer classes in midlife, ran his own finance and insurance business, and, most importantly, he never stopped being curious.

Our Sunday afternoons together remind me of *The Power of One*, because I'm issued one beer, one cup of coffee, and one steak. The steak is the size of a dinner plate. But the really important side dish is his question of the week. My grandfather spends all week ruminating on something he wants to ask me. We work through our *Power of One* rations and then—here we go.

The conversation always starts like this. He leans back in his chair, twiddling a toothpick as he looks over at me. "Now," he says, taking a deep breath for emphasis, "I have a question for you."

What kinds of questions do you think a perpetually curious 96-year-old might ask? His questions touch on topics like: "How does the Internet work?" "What is 'the cloud'?" He wonders how companies make money on this "cloud," wherever it may be. "What does it mean to live 'off the grid,' " he asks, and "How are we ever going to pay off this national debt?"

I'll never forget the time I had the opportunity to accompany him on a flight to Washington, D.C., to honor the sacrifices of World War II veterans. While most of the vets sat in their seats, having polite conversation, my grandfather verbally dismantled every part of the plane, because he was curious about how things worked.

My grandfather spends his time day trading using his smartwatch, his two iPads, and multiple laptops. He poses questions to Siri (affectionately calling her, "Sirrah") about what he might do next. Every Sunday, he tests me, but Sirrah gets it every day. Evidently, he wants to know what she knows, as he continues to look for the edge of the Internet.

It's fascinating to me that no matter how much he's learned and no matter how much he's experienced, he's always interested in asking more questions. He's determined never to stop making discoveries. Born before the Great Depression, he's lived through world wars, moon landings, and the microwave. What you and I might consider "archival footage" is simply his life. His memories. His personal perspective.

Think of all that he's seen and experienced! What would happen if you could capture the power of his curiosity and bring that to life in your business? What questions would you ask if you realized that there was always something new to discover?

When we are curious, the journey never ends. You don't have to wait until Sunday to find out something fascinating about the world and the people in it. In business, as in life, there's always a question waiting to be discovered. The better questions lead to the best discoveries, but only if you have the courage to ask. Those questions are always an invitation—an invitation to discover something new. Something about yourself . . . your world . . . your possibilities.

So many times, when we listen—to customers or to each other—we listen to *affirm*. We design questions and inquiry in a way that reaffirms our beliefs, instead of exploring new possibilities. Why? What if questions could become tools to go beyond affirmation of what you already know—about your customers and your business—and open up new possibilities?

By 2020, customer experience will overtake price and product as the key brand differentiator, according to Smart Think (https://bit.ly/listenup -smartthink). And in a Helpscout report (https://bit.ly/listenup-healthscout), satisfied clients resulted in a 30 percent increased profitability for a business, as they were 80 percent more likely to renew their services. Nearly 90 percent of business buyers expect companies to understand their business needs and expectations, according to data compiled by Salesforce (https://bit.ly /listenup-connectedcustomer). There is an urgent, powerful, and compelling need to find out what those needs and expectations are. Affirming what you already know isn't going to build your business.

Real innovation is a defining factor for two-thirds of business buyers, according to Salesforce research; 66 percent of customers actively seek to buy from the most innovative companies. What if asking so-called "risky" questions is the most effective way for uncovering the actual risks that your company faces? If your leadership fails to ask the questions that lead to new discoveries, how can you compete? Your organization may join the ranks of Kodak, Nokia, and Blockbuster in the Land of Lost Innovation.

> The marvelous thing about a good question is that it shapes our identity as much by the asking as it does by the answering.
>
> *David Whyte, English Poet*

In his book, *Leading with Questions: How Leaders Find the Right Solutions by Knowing What to Ask* (Jossey-Bass, 2014), author Michael Marquardt explains the dilemma like this:

> When we become leaders, we of course want to be the one with the answers rather than the one with questions. One of the most difficult challenges you may have as a leader is to accept that you may not know what is right, or best, for most situations. We have become accustomed to having the right answers, so it's hard to let go of the answer-providing habit. We want to protect our self-image and our image in the eyes of others; we also want to protect ourselves from uncomfortable feelings such as fear. Exposing ourselves with questions offers risks on all these fronts.

The ability to make new discoveries is predicated on the letting go of preconceptions. Instead of seeking affirmation, or rushing to provide an answer, Marquardt says that something more important is needed—Courage.

Courage includes the willingness to ask questions that may challenge—or even break up—current perceptions and patterns.

Imagine if you brought a child to a business dinner. What would that child hear? And say? I discovered the answers (and more) when one of the senior executives had a childcare snafu just before a customer-listening dinner. So he brought a "plus one" to the meeting. Sitting politely and quietly at the end of the table, seven-year-old Isabella played with her menu, some Legos®, and a coloring book. Meanwhile, the customer-listening dinner continued uninterrupted. We talked about technology, cross-functional challenges, and the social impact of some new manufacturing processes.

We're two hours deep into this dialogue and there's a lull in the conversation. Isabella puts down her crayon and says to the group, "Do you think you'll fix this by the time I grow up?"

Every head turned. Chuckles came from some parts of the table. She started coloring again and spoke as she looked down at the motion of her crayon, "I wonder how hard this really is."

Her dad snickered as he shook his head. He shifted around in his chair, just a little.

"Aren't you all just saying the same thing?" she said, looking at her dad now, as his squirming visibly increased. "There's too much talking, and not enough listening and you need to talk to the people who are getting the benefit of these program thingies and, if you listen to them, they will tell you what to do." She paused. "You don't have to figure it out all by yourself."

Boom.

OUT OF THE MOUTHS OF BABES

Isabella summarized the whole event scenario in three sentences:

- Stop talking to each other.
- Stop talking over each other.
- You don't have to go it alone.

We listened. Not just because we are polite, but because she was right. If we stopped talking to each other, we might go out and talk to someone who could really offer some insight: our customers.

Little Isabella had courage—and surprising insight.

But she also had something beyond outspoken bravery, or impulsiveness. I'm talking about a unique superpower that all children seem to possess, and most grown-ups seem to dismiss. She had *curiosity,* a deep natural curiosity to explore new solutions. On many levels, that's what being a kid is all about—exploring. That fresh perspective is the beginner's mindset. We've talked about it before. From courage and curiosity, new discoveries can be made.

The child's mind is open to explore in ways that often adults do not. The child's perspective is that every idea and every piece of feedback is potentially valid. A kid doesn't automatically discount someone's point of view. Adults are different: We're numb to hearing things, so we just stop listening. When we think we know it all, we never ask for more. That approach reinforces preconceptions. Adults fail to see the fun—the potential discovery—inside every conversation.

Looking past preconceptions in a big way isn't childish. It's effective. The child's mind sees things with fresh eyes and hears things with fresh ears. It's counterintuitive, but the most mature and sophisticated position you can take (when it comes to asking customer questions) is the beginner's mindset.

But mindset alone isn't enough to hear your customers in new ways. Curiosity and courage are important. Beyond this, there's one other thing that you need if you're going to open up the conversation: Context.

For example, consider Chicago engineer Marty Cooper (https://bit.ly/listenup-martycooper). In the 1970s, he asked a strange and never-before-considered question: "Why is it that when we call a person, we have to call one specific place?" In 1973, Marty's employer, Motorola, became the first company to launch mobile phone service—the ability to call any place from every place, really. The first mobile phone call was made by none other than Marty Cooper, the Alexander Graham Bell of the digital age. His company had invested in a culture of discovery—the context for Cooper's curiosity. Ultimately, his inquiry was rewarded and the whole world changed.

What questions could you ask, right now, that could change your world? What's the context that you need for the change you seek?

When I was leading a global team, one of my employees was based in South Africa. When you think of South Africa, what comes to mind? Do you really have a context for understanding South Africa and what that country's culture means to the day-to-day lives of the people who live there?

South Africa: I was familiar, but I wasn't fully informed. Have you ever experienced that feeling? You need to connect across social, political, and geographic boundaries. You need insight into someone else's world. But what's the best and fastest way to establish the kind of rapport that's really going to matter?

I knew we probably weren't going to be spending a lot of time together in person, so talking with my new team member took on an elevated importance. In the process of getting acquainted, I asked her about her life, her family, and her interests. But here's when the conversation became really interesting.

"If every American only knew one thing about South Africa," I asked her, "what would you want it to be?"

The answer, she told me, was already inside my question. By asking for a new perspective, I did what most Americans did not. I listened. From a place of genuine curiosity, I learned what the world looked like from her vantage point. Her response to my inquiries revealed cultural differences and insights that went far beyond where her kids went to school or what the weather is like in Durban in December. Her answer imparted knowledge not only of how things work in South Africa, but of how key cultural differences are rarely explored by most Americans. I learned more about her and her lifestyle in her answer than through any other topic we could have discussed, because I didn't just hear her words: I understood her perspective.

When you think about listening to the customer, there's a valuable and powerful question that needs to be asked. If you have the courage and the curiosity, the context is incredibly revealing.

Ask your customer: "What's *our* biggest misperception about *our* business?"

The voice of your customer is a mirror—look into it.

Just because we have information (data), we think we know what's really going on. And maybe we do. But the beginner's mind seeks to confirm suspicions and explore curiosities. What's the real context for the data? Crossing the digital divide, we unite in the brave pursuit of new discoveries.

> If you do not know how to ask the right question, you discover nothing.
>
> *W. Edwards Deming, Father of the Japanese Post-War Economic Revolution*

Remember that trended answers to questions are never as powerful as the narrative itself. Data informs, but customer conversations create insight. Take time to be curious about the context for the data.

Tim Hockey, CEO of TD Ameritrade, tells *Forbes* (https://bit.ly/listenup -ameritrade) that winning the client experience is the company's top priority. Beaumont Vance is the company's director of AI, Chat, and Emerging Technology. He's using AI to capture, analyze, and interpret millions of call center conversations, leveraging NLP (Natural Language Processing) systems to capture the customer journey. Why go to the trouble of converting millions of conversations into transcripts and then diving deep into those conversations? Curiosity. And context. Vance figures that there is 500 percent more information in customer calls than in the traditional analytical data. The back-and-forth around questions reveals powerful insights for Vance and his team.

Which would you rather have: a two-way customer conversation or a one-way score? Sure, you got a 4.6, but are you winning? For Hockey and Vance, the goal is more than a score. TD Ameritrade wants to serve customers better by better understanding what drives their actions and sentiment.

Delivering the commencement speech at Northwestern University (https://bit.ly/listenup-wildcats), former IBM CEO Ginni Rometty said, "Instead of artificial intelligence, I think we'll augment our intelligence. It will not be a world of man versus machine. It will be a world of man plus machines." Is that formula adding up to new results within your organization?

What's driving data is the story behind it. Consider how narrative—the customers' tales told in their own words—can give life to statistics and numbers. In *Mind and Nature: A Necessary Unity* (Hampton Press, 2002), author Gregory Bateson hypothesized a possible dialogue between man and machine:

A man wanted to know about mind, not in nature, but in his private large computer. He asked [his computer], "Do you compute that you will ever think like a human being?" The machine then set to work to analyze its own computational habits. Finally, the machine printed its answer on a piece of paper, as such machines do. The man ran to get the answer and found, neatly typed, the words:
THAT REMINDS ME OF A STORY

C-SPARKS: I've Got Some Questions for You

Let's look at some of the top questions that can help you to open up the conversation and make valuable discoveries. While not intended as a checklist, these questions can help you check in on new customer insights. Which one do you like the best and which one would serve your customers the most?

IF I COULD ONLY DELIVER ONE MESSAGE TO OUR TOP EXECUTIVES ON YOUR BEHALF, WHAT WOULD IT BE?

Do you know what matters most to your customers? That's the answer that they will provide if this question is asked with sincerity. And it works as a single survey question. It works after an event takes place. It works to close a meeting with a customer. Or a series of them. For organizations, over 80 percent of companies expect to compete mainly based on CX (customer experience), according to Gartner (https://gtnr.it/2WzzSPW). Want to help your leadership team to compete? Ask your customers about the one thing that you need to know. This open-ended question is powerful on three levels:

- It lends itself easily to extracting stories, and it is great for pulling representative quotes.
- The question points toward what it is you're not asking but should be. If multiple respondents comment on "ease of doing business," but none of your customer interactions involve questions around ease of doing business, you're missing an opportunity. Find what's top of mind from your customer's point of view (POV).
- Key themes will jump out: Count how many times a theme or phrase shows up, either manually or using automated tools. Does this repeated sentiment reflect a complaint, problem, or possibility? Whatever your answer, you've just discovered a blind spot.

(continued)

(continued)

WHAT ARE WE MISSING?

Salesforce Research surveyed over 6,700 consumers and business buyers globally to understand better the modern customer mindset. According to the Salesforce research (https://bit.ly/listenup-statista), nearly 70 percent of customers set the importance of the experience higher than ever. Doesn't it make sense to find out what those higher expectations actually are? The point of the question is to gain context, since 70 percent of customers say that they expect connected experiences in which their preferences are known across touchpoints. This open-ended question can show you whether your touchpoints are making a mark—or missing it.

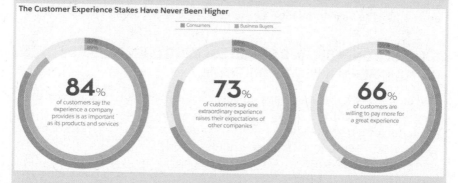

The Customer Experience Stakes Have Never Been Higher

■ Consumers   ■ Business Buyers

84% of customers say the experience a company provides is as important as its products and services

73% of customers say one extraordinary experience raises their expectations of other companies

66% of customers are willing to pay more for a great experience

WHO DOES THIS BETTER THAN WE DO AND WHY?

In *Leading with Questions*, Marquardt explains, "Leaders who can ask, process information, and learn in a highly efficient manner will build organizations that have a tremendous competitive advantage over their slower and less proactive competition."

Think you know who your competition is? Better ask your customer. And don't be afraid to look outside your current industry for answers. Customers may describe a company with great customer service that's in another industry. Don't discount that valuable piece of information, even if it means investigating a company that you don't consider to be a competitor today! Find out about their practices so that you can fit them into yours! This information can be a tool for competitive advantage, disruption, and more. Taking a limited view of your industry and your competitors isn't going to help you expand and innovate. Innovation lies with best-of-breed companies, and maybe—just maybe—those best practices are found outside of your industry. Are you willing to look?

IF WE COULD ONLY DELIVER ON ONE OF YOUR ASKS OR IDEAS, WHICH WOULD BE MOST IMPORTANT?

Insights into priorities can keep you from playing the role of a genie. Finding new solutions isn't always about granting wishes: explore what matters most to your customer. You can always ask the $100 question, either of your customers or of your leadership team: "If you only had $100 to spend on the initiatives we've just discussed, how would you allocate it?"

Of course, $100 isn't enough to create transformational change around a business process. But it's a start. So where would you put your money? Would you drop all $100 on a new software program? Invest in training? Develop a new offsite for the leadership team? Or what exactly? Divide and conquer by allocating your resources toward what matters most.

IF WE COULD CREATE "X" FOR YOU, WOULD YOU CONSIDER US A VIABLE RESOURCE OR PARTNER?

If you see yourself as a leader in your industry, that's great. But does the customer agree with your assessment? The best questions don't just look at perception; they inquire about intention. This question points toward the perception around your organization. If you come out with a new whizbang gadget but your customers don't see your company as a viable player in that market sector, your investment in R&D might be misplaced! Don't you want to know whether your multimillion-dollar investment is built around a viable thirsty customer instead of just relying on your own product roadmap? After all, if the journey isn't useful, believable, and compelling, the customer won't go there with you.

WHAT WOULD MAKE YOU CONSIDER US?

According to the *Harvard Business Review* (https://bit.ly/listenup-hbrquestions), scientific research dating back to the 1970s shows that people have conversations to accomplish two things: information exchange and impression management. Notice that this question isn't about impression management (liking). Instead, the question points at the

(continued)

(continued)

tangible exchange of information (learning) that can help you to get a seat at the customer's table. In this article by Refract Resources (https://bit.ly/listenup-discovery), author Kevin Beales shares how, in a discovery call, every question and answer has to move the needle to create fit—or qualify where fit doesn't exist. This question provides a rich opportunity for discovery about the customer's aspirations, wishes, and wants. More importantly, are there some perception barriers around your organization? For example, are you aspiring to be a company that doesn't appear viable from the customer's standpoint? This question can reveal what makes your prospect "sticky." Why are they loyal to somebody else? And what would you have to do to be considered as an in-demand alternative?

WHAT COULD WE WORK ON/WHAT ARE YOU WORKING ON THAT'S EXCITING TO YOU?

In our modern culture, people are focused on expansive opportunities, possibilities, and potential—not nuisance, nagging, and anguish. True, all people (and organizations) have difficulties, shortcomings, and challenges. But what's the line of questioning that will open up the dialogue about where your customer is headed? Pointing people toward pain is never as enticing or informative as asking about what excites them. In *Drive: The Surprising Truth About What Motivates Us* (Riverhead Books, 2009), author Daniel Pink explains his idea of Motivation 3.0—the drivers that really govern desire in today's modern workplace. He points to three areas: Autonomy, Mastery, and Purpose. Pink explains, "The most deeply motivated people—not to mention those who are most productive and satisfied—have desires to help a cause larger than themselves." Where's the pain in that? Have you found your customer's higher cause? Have you considered the "why" behind your customers' interaction with you? The only thing that hurts is if your organization is seeking some mythical "ouch," instead of what really motivates the people who buy your products.

HOW DOES THIS INITIATIVE (STILL) FIT ON YOUR PRIORITY LIST?

I used to work with a guy whose favorite management question was, "Where are we?" The question pointed toward accountability and relevance—reinforcing alignment or identifying where it was missing. Understanding the relevance of your organization (inside of your customer's context) is the most valuable location service you can find, because if what you're working on doesn't matter to your customer, it doesn't matter. Ever had something that was superimportant one quarter become an ignored memory in the next one? It happens all the time. That's why this question is so vital: Tune in to where your customer is right now. Needs change, goals shift, and priorities splinter. If you don't know where you are in terms of a customer's priorities, you're not one.

The greatest gift is not being afraid to question.
Ruby Dee, Actress and Civil Rights Activist

Instead of just scanning existing feedback, get curious. Observation isn't the end of the journey; current data points toward the questions that you still need to ask. Asking better questions is easy—even a child can do it.

Question everything.
Albert Einstein

True genius starts with questioning what you already know. Then follow that question with others that can help you to unlock that beginner's mind-set. Turn brave inquiry to your customer's context, finding the courage and the curiosity to change the conversation, because if you won't, your competition will.

A powerful question still unanswered is a Genius Question. Businesses will thrive or die based on the answer to the Genius Question, because it's the single most powerful tool in building your future. Are you ready to add a touch of genius to your customers' experience?

In the next chapter, we'll look at the inquiry that will tame your competition and keep your customers craving more. The Genius Question is waiting for you and your customers. Do you know what it is?

CHAPTER 8

Got Genius?

What was I thinking?

If you've ever moved, you've asked yourself that question. Changing houses or apartments is never easy. Disruption can cause you to question your choices. Your sanity. Your sense of direction.

I knew something was up even before my moving day arrived. I had been getting quotes from several movers in town, preparing to transition from the suburbs to the city. The third company I called sent Mr. Byron Jackson over. He brought a clipboard, an attention to detail, and over 40 years of experience to the conversation.

Byron opened every cabinet and every drawer, asked me about where I had bought certain furniture pieces. While the other movers were interested in my stuff, Byron was invested.

He took nearly two hours longer than anyone else, with a level of thoroughness that left me feeling a sense of calm. Clearly, he cared about my move at a level that seemed to rival my own. That intention made my choice easy: I bet on Byron and hired his company, Stuart's Moving and Storage.

In 1936, Marion Stuart decided to open a moving company that was dedicated to local Indianapolis residents, according to the company website. With one small truck and a single employee, Marion entered the world of entrepreneurship. As an African American during this era, Marion's business undertaking was a leap of faith that took both dedication and courage. Marion shared that dedication and business savvy with his nephew, Anthony Stuart. For many years the two worked together to make Stuart's Moving and Storage, Inc., the company that it is today. In the late 1960s, Anthony took the reins from his uncle, dedicating his life to the relocation industry. Today, at the helm of the company, Anthony is a very hands-on CEO.

As I was about to find out.

MOVING DAY: ENTERING THE UNKNOWN

On a hot July day, my doorbell rang. Stuart's Moving and Storage had arrived. Roy and Thaddeus introduced themselves. Together, they would be directing the team, and they wanted to get started right away.

But first they had an unexpected question: What kind of music do you like? Because they were going to play that kind of music all day long while they loaded my stuff. Before they began boxing, they unboxed a few items of their own.

To make it even easier for me to clean up my existing house, they brought me Swiffer® pads and other cleaning supplies. They handed me a thick set of folded boxes, so that I could pack the personal items that I would take in my car to my new place. I received a total care package; they had anticipated my needs (including my musical tastes).

Then they pulled out another box.

Inside were one dozen of the most amazing donuts I've ever had in my life. Right out of the gate, moving was absolutely delicious. "Don't forget to check the card," Thaddeus said, as he grabbed a chair from the dining room.

I opened it instantly, revealing a beautiful hand-crafted message.

"Working with you" it said on the outside, "has moved us."

It was signed by everyone who had spoken to me so far on my move, from Byron to the guys in my house who had just grabbed three lamps and a sofa. I smiled as I watched them quickly dash out to the curb with my couch. I turned the card over for a personal message from Anthony Stuart. It read, in part, "If you are not completely satisfied with our work to this point, for any reason, please contact me directly." His mobile phone number was at the bottom of the message.

The day wore on; the heat was brutal. The guys were trying their best, but they were running behind. Five o'clock came and went. I was starting to calculate what the overtime was going to cost me when the phone rang.

"Karen, hi, hey, it's Anthony. Anthony Stuart from Stuart's Moving. How are you holding up? I know it's been a long day. Are you doing alright?"

I was stunned. I wasn't sure how to answer him. I think I mentioned something about how I knew the guys were doing the best they could. There was a knock on the door. "Hold on," I said, as I reached for the doorknob.

The door opened to reveal three more Stuart's employees. The cavalry had arrived. As they scurried between the porch and the truck, they all waved hello.

I could tell Anthony was saying something, so I turned my attention back to the phone ". . . should be there by now. The guys will help you get this done, so we don't run into tomorrow morning. And Karen, don't worry about any extra charges. We said we'd get you moved today, and we're gonna do just that.

No overtime, no extra labor. Hang in there—we're in this with you, and we're not gonna stop 'til the job is done."

By the time they left, all my stuff was in the new house. It was 11 p.m.

As I shut the door to my new place, I realized: I was absolutely starving.

Let me tell you, leftover donuts have never tasted so good. The gooey glaze —the result of the hot summer day—made them taste better than many of the three-star Michelin meals I've enjoyed. For the life of me, I can't remember the name of the folks that made those donuts. But I'll never forget the team that delivered them.

Even though the job took longer in the heat and additional resources were needed, Stuart's held to their pricing estimate. At every turn, they made a difficult journey easier. As a result, I've recommended them to several friends, and their experiences have echoed my own.

Moving is never easy. Research shows that moving is right up there with a death in the family in terms of stressfulness. Weather and other complications can make moving to a new house even more difficult. But Stuart's Moving and Storage was relentless about reducing the stress.

I was uneasy about the move. They worked hard to make it easy by joining me on my journey. They anticipated my needs along the way. They delivered on their promises, even when extra resources and expenses were required.

Their approach was nothing short of genius.

Because, if you're really a genius, things are easier for you. So, by extension, when you share your company's genius, you make doing business easier. A genius business is one that can crush customer stress, overcome market obstacles, and clarify hidden expectations at every turn.

Ready to tap into your genius? Then ask yourself—and ask your customers—the Genius Question:

What could we do to make this easier for you?

Maybe you're wondering why I didn't say, "make this easy for you"?

"Easy" may look like a destination, but it's not.

"Easy," to be quite frank, is a destination you and your customer may never reach together.

Easier is a journey.

Easier is what you can influence.

Easier is where you need to look.

I believe there is no "best," only better.

Akio Toyoda, CEO of Toyota

Like the word "easy," the word "best" implies that you've arrived. You can stop now because you're the best. But on the path of quality, customer satisfaction, and growth, the journey must go on. Built on a foundation of kaizen (continuous improvement), the drive for improvement is (wait for it) continuous. Because you can always be better. And your customer doesn't want to wait for it.

If you're in a heavily regulated industry (like finance, healthcare, energy, or air travel, or maybe we'd better just say "business" and call it a day) where someone else is setting the rules, your customer's life may never be easy. When there are strict guidelines you have to follow (safety, confidentiality, permits, government process, and so forth) "easy" is more of a theoretical concept. An aspiration. But not a destination.

Moving is not "easy." But it was easier than I ever expected. When you ask the genius question, you can exceed your customer's expectations—not set unrealistic ones.

The word "easier" looks in the direction of truth. Face it: Your customer's journey may never be easy. But maybe you can take a couple steps out of the process. Or reduce the number of clicks to access relevant product information on your website. Or reduce the number of times that customers have to call you back.

Take the mattress on your bed as an example. You know that you're supposed to flip that thing every so often. No matter how strong you are, if you try to do it yourself it's not easy. Maneuvering what's underneath your fitted sheet is tough! It'll fold up on you and knock over your nightstand before you get it turned around. But when you get somebody to help you, it's not quite so awkward. It's still gonna bend on you (and you better watch out for that lamp on your dresser), but two people can make an uneasy task easier by working together towards a common goal.

Stop searching for easy. Think about the customer's journey and how to make it easier. An "easier" focus will impact how you listen, serve, and drive value. Because you can always make it easier. Always.

FINDING GENIUS

Can anyone access genius?

We think of genius as being grandiose and elevated and elite. When we talk about genius, what comes to mind? "I'm not Einstein. My idea is probably not that genius."

Let me clarify a misunderstanding.

Think of a time, right now, when you had a moment of insight. Of wisdom. Of genius.

Guess what? We've all got at least one story where we figured something out—a story of where we tapped into resources that we didn't know we had; where we found the thing that was missing.

Looking back, you may think, "Oh, what was missing was so obvious!" But before you found it, it was still missing! That's what insight is: seeing the thing that was hidden before or seeing things in a new way. Benjamin Franklin didn't "discover" electricity. It was always there. But his insights into what is now "obvious" power that lamp on your desk.

Anyone can be a genius. You don't need a PhD or a superhigh IQ. Because you've got DNA. The ability to think things through in new ways is like five fingers on a hand: It's built into the original operating system that we all share.

Brilliance comes to all of us, sometimes when we least expect it. The real question is: Will you recognize it when it shows up? Will you share what you see? Your insight could be the one that changes everything.

I used to think that genius, like success, was something that was reserved for somebody else—someone "out there." You know, "those people." The successful people. The geniuses.

Then I realized something. Success is like genius—we all can access it. Maybe your genius is not the same as mine, or Sam's, or Susan's, but we have moments of genius. Of success. Of insight.

The right answer—the answer that makes it easier—is out there. Who says it won't be you who finds a genius idea? Who sees what others might have missed?

One thing is for certain: until you seek, you will never find.

Your customers are seeking an easier way. If you don't join them on this quest, your competitors will. Every company has something that makes it difficult for their customers to do business with them. The specifics are discovered when customers fail to renew, when calls come into customer service, when customers call the CEO directly (or the chairman's hotline or the complaint line), and through open-ended questions. Customers typically point to processes that aren't efficient, have a large number of approvers, or have too many steps. The conflict can be too many clicks to log a customer service case, too many signoffs to close a contract, too much time to receive a refund, and more.

Almost always, ease points to a gap between expectation and execution. If the customer expects that a contract will take a week and it takes a month, there's a gap between expectation and execution. Your scores and your business will suffer as a result.

The mistake that most companies make is trying to solve for all things at once. The problem is that you'll be tackling everything from customer rebates to world peace. Where do you begin?

If everything's important, then nothing is.

There are two ways to solve the complexity puzzle: One is to do a key driver analysis. It's a statistics tool that helps you assess the correlation between the factor and how much it drives overall perception. And if you uncover 10 items, for example, you can statistically correlate how much an individual item on the to-do list impacts the overall perception of "easy to do business with" or "likelihood to renew."

The other way to simplify the process is to ask customers and employees about quick wins. You're asking two sets of customers (internal and external) how to make it (whatever "it" is) easier. And you can unlock follow-up questions like: "How could we solve support cases more easily/quickly?" or "What's the one business process that we have that slows you down and just doesn't seem to make sense?"

Moments of genius are often about what we can remove, not what we can add. That's what *Top Chef*'s Christina Tosi discovered.

Do you know what all great chefs have in common? Regardless of style or food category, every great chef always serves one thing that makes his or her style unforgettable. Here's the special ingredient they all use: nostalgia.

Great food instantly transports you back to a simpler time. The greatest chefs in the world aren't making boeuf bourguignon, risotto, tiramisu, or soufflés. They are making memories.

The taste of the past is what saved the restaurant in the movie, *Ratatouille*. The title dish created a reminiscence in the mind of the hard-hearted food critic, transporting him to a simpler time. The true artist in the kitchen mixes ingredients and temperature to create something that goes beyond taste and nutrition. The chef, at his or her peak of genius, creates a memory.

David Chang, founder of the Momofuku dynasty in New York City, says that Christina Tosi is a genius at creating nostalgia. From her early work with business partner Chang, Tosi went on to found Milk Bar, one of the most highly regarded dessert restaurants in the world. A James Beard award winner and a cohost on Top Chef, the 38-year-old Tosi is widely regarded as one of the foremost pastry chefs in the world.

How did she tap into her genius?

Here's how she describes her innovative take on a childhood staple on *Chef's Table* (Netflix, Season 4, Episode 1):

"Cake is the thing that you're raised as a child in America to be like the most exciting, most celebratory dessert you can have, and it was . . . okay."

Christina Tosi wrinkles her nose at the thought of traditional birthday cake. "It's spongy. It usually doesn't have that much flavor. It's usually a little dry. There's not a lot of texture. Just like a world of missed opportunities. Yes, I knew . . . that cake could be a lot better than what it was.

"From being in culinary school, around all of these insane masters of beauty and perfection when it comes to finishing a cake, they had tired me out completely." Christina got to the point where she said, *"I don't think cakes should be frosted. I've seen how obsessed you can get with frosting a cake, and that time should be spent elsewhere."*

What could make this easier?

"Time should be spent in the actual layers of cake or frostings or fillings or whatever it is, but it shouldn't be spent on a turntable, trying to make the perfect, perfect, PERFECT frosted cake. For what? We're not in pottery class."

> **NOTE**
>
> In professional kitchens, the sides of a cake are frosted on a Lazy Susan, a spinning plate that resembles a pottery wheel. As a chef myself, I can tell you how difficult it is to navigate a spatula around the sides of a spinning cake. I've mastered the technique, but often I've wished that there were a way to make this task easier!

"When I start to think about all of these different moments and decisions and time and work put into making the most delicious cake . . . and cake soak and frosting and crumb and filling, well . . . why would I cover it up?" Christina asks. *"It was that dollhouse moment of looking in and being like, 'I want to see the world of amazing things that's happening on the inside.'"*

Guess what? Cake without icing on the sides is still delicious. In the hands of a master chef, a new level of transparency (seeing the layers; seeing inside) became the process. As an expert trained in the French culinary traditions, Christina Tosi certainly knows how to frost a cake. When she looked beyond her training, she wasn't trying to cut corners. She wanted to expose something new. Something unexpected.

Her genius showed up when she left something out. By taking something away, Christina Tosi revealed her genius.

What could you take away from your traditional process? What could you remove to create greater transparency for your customers? When was the last time you took a hard look at the layers in your organization and built in real transparency?

Tosi exposed the traditional dish, instead of hiding it. Along the way, she exposed all of America to new ways of experiencing birthday cake.

Tosi's genius moment—tapping into a memory and revealing something familiar in a new way—made it easier than ever to uncover a new sensation. If you haven't had her birthday cake, take it from me: it is truly sensational.

In an interview with William Best (https://bit.ly/listenup-tosi), Tosi explains her process: "A lot of the things that I make at Milk Bar are things that are traditionally American, as a form, but that I could never quite fall in love with myself. I love pie, in theory, but I felt like pie needed to be challenged." It was this line of reasoning that led her to create "Crack Pie," another signature dish.

> **NOTE**
>
> What's a tradition within your business that you aren't necessarily in love with? What tried-and-true ideas in your company could benefit from challenge, inquiry, and exploration?

Challenging the status quo can help you to tap into your own genius . . . your own insight . . . your own ability to see things in new ways.

> *"I think the world is more often your oyster when you approach it with more of a childlike sensibility," Tosi says on* Chef's Table, *as she explains what happens when the beginner's mindset meets the genius question. "The world is a more curious place. It's a more beautiful place. It's not always sunshine and rainbows, but within any given day in life, there should always be a moment where the weight of the world is just a little bit lighter on your shoulders."*

And lighter for your customers as well. Consider the recipe that Tosi followed to tap into her genius:

1. She used common ingredients to create uncommon results.
2. She wasn't afraid to challenge the basis of culture (you've heard of "American Pie," right?) and rethink nostalgia.

3. What she took away and left out was exactly what revealed her genius.

Have you ever stopped to consider the opposite of genius? I don't mean the antonym. I'm talking about what opposes your genius. What gets in the way? What do you know and recognize that's NOT fueling your genius? Here's what strikes me as the opposite of genius:

1. **Superstition.** That's another way of saying the seven most dangerous words in all of business, "That's the way we've always done things." Superstition is a widely held but completely unjustified belief. Superstition is the connection of coincidence and unrelated events, based on supposition and turned into a mantra . . . or company culture. Superstitions create artificial boundaries, limitations, and misunderstandings. Don't believe me? Here, pet this adorable black cat. You may believe that it will bring you bad luck, but actually it's just purring. You make your own luck when you turn away from superstition.
2. **Rules and Regulations.** Is it any wonder that *First, Break All the Rules: What the World's Greatest Managers Do Differently* (Gallup Press, 2016) sat on the best-seller list for 93 weeks when it was released? Launching the writing career of Marcus Buckingham, this title pointed to the genius in creating employee engagement. Genius doesn't come from rules. Rules come from genius. Get the order right, and your customers will thank you for it. I'm not suggesting that anarchy is a good business strategy. But seeing beyond "the way we've always done things" is the first place to look if you want to make life easier for your customers.
3. **Habits.** If you wish to uncover a new way of looking at your business, your process, and your customers, habits won't help you. At its core, moments of genius are moments of discovery.

But get this: Genius can become a habit.

At least, that's what I've seen from a certain trailblazer, a leader I respect and admire, who has created a culture where genius can thrive. I'm talking about none other than Salesforce founder and CEO, Marc Benioff.

Marc has made genius a habit, and he has created a culture in which genius can thrive. Marc has done something better than any big company executive I've experienced in the B2B space: He has created a place where people belong. Win or lose, team members at Salesforce feel that they're part of something bigger than themselves. Something that matters. And that feeling transfers to our customers, our partners, and the entire community that's touched by Salesforce's products and people.

Trust is the underlying thread of genius for Marc. The importance of trust is a driving force in every stakeholder interaction, and it permeates the culture of the company.

In Marc's most recent book, *Trailblazer: The Power of Business as the Greatest Platform for Change* (Currency, 2019), and in multiple speeches, he calls it the "value of values."

Marc explains it this way:

> *"The gap between what customers really want from businesses and what's really possible is vanishing rapidly. The future isn't about learning to be better at doing what we already do, it's about **how far we can stretch the boundaries of our imagination** [emphasis mine]. We have to resist the urge to make quick, marginal improvements and spend more time listening deeply to what customers really want, even if they're not fully aware of it yet."*

Marc is not afraid to say what others won't: I'm talking about his open call for greater regulation of tech companies. In an interview with CNN's Laurie Segall (https://bit.ly/listenup-benioff), Marc said:

> *"Facebook is the new nicotine. It's not good for you: You don't know who's trying to convince you to use it or misuse it. . . . We need regulation in this industry," he says, indicting himself and his peers. "I don't trust this industry to self-regulate."*

Is this CEO shooting himself in the foot, or the head, or both? Calling for regulation? Isn't that the exact opposite of what a CEO should want?

But consider this point of view: What's going to make it easier *for the customers*?

Doing the right thing isn't always easier. In fact, the right thing to do is often the hard thing to do. But calling for regulation is not about what makes things difficult for Salesforce, or other technology companies, or any company in general. There's something greater at stake—trust.

> *"Over the years, I've learned that trust and transparency are two sides of the same coin," Marc explains in* Trailblazer. *"As CEO, I could lay all our company secrets—all our code, all our financial data, all our technical troubles—out for all our employees to see, but if those employees can't count on one another, no amount of openness on the part of management will be enough. The people in the trenches need to be able to trust that their team, and their leaders, will be right there on the ground, working beside them, when the going gets tough."*

He continues, "I won't try to deny that when you put yourself out there, there's usually some pain involved. Vulnerability is scary. But it also makes you stronger."

Leadership isn't easy, especially as expectations have shifted. Customers want to do business with a company that understands values, transparency, and trust.

According to Marc, "Acting as responsible corporate citizens is the right thing to do, because consumers demand it."

Are you ready to bring your values to life? It might look like you're going to have to work harder to deliver what your customers expect. But look again.

Work smarter. It's easier.

Don't be satisfied with incremental improvements. Instead, explore imagination. Possibility. Cocreate with your customers. Don't just talk about values: live them. Take the frosting off your proverbial cake. Stretch your boundaries to create greater transparency than ever before.

Ask the genius question about your values, your team, your processes: What could we do to make this easier for you?

And don't stop being curious.

When you engage in that kind of leadership, you encourage your employees and your customers to be a part of something that maybe—just maybe—shows a spark of true genius.

CHAPTER 9

Genius, Revealed

With a few clicks and a credit card, a surprise was in the making.

Except that surprise wasn't the one I anticipated.

It was my brother's birthday, and I wanted to buy him a special gift.

The only present he received from me was an email from the company's customer service team: "We're sorry your gift won't be delivered by the date we promised."

Missed dates and deadlines are understandable, but this story will explain how our relationship ended. (Not my relationship with my brother, but my relationship with this vendor.)

Two days before his birthday, I was on the phone. The delivery date was that day. I needed an update. I exchanged pleasantries with my service rep and dove in.

"Where's the package?" I heard the click clack of typing. The smartphone sat face up on my desk, speakerphone button highlighted in blue. The simple email from my brother was still on my screen. Four words glowed on the monitor. "Sorry sis, no packages." The late afternoon sun was streaming through the blinds in my office. The clicking didn't stop. I wondered whether the sun would set before I had any real answers. How could this be so difficult?

"We are not certain of the exact whereabouts of your package," Amy explained in a soothing, please-step-away-from-the-ledge voice.

"Well, how do we find it?" Amy was my assigned account rep (because I buy that much stuff from her company). Because shipping is simple, I'd never had to speak with her until today.

"It's not that simple," Amy explained. "Because we use a third-party shipper, we're not really responsible for that information." On my desk was a brightly colored laser cut card, lying on top of an envelope the golden color of a wheat field. At least I will be able to give him this card in person, I thought to myself. Downstairs in the kitchen was my wooden wine rack, filled with multiple bottles of wine. None was as nice as the one I was trying to order. Yet there they sat, like resting soldiers in wine-rack bunks, ready to be called into action.

Amy's voice broke the silence. "Maybe you could call the shipping company yourself?"

What?

I wanted answers. I got homework.

Have you been there? Have you ever had a customer service rep ask you to investigate one of their vendor relationships?

I looked in the mirror for confirmation: Yes, I was the customer. Who was serving whom here?

I'm guessing you've done this dance. You see something online. You place an order. It doesn't show up, and the company tells you to go fix it. Even if you are a longtime customer (I was) and you have an assigned rep (hi, Amy), you end up at a surprise party that no one wants to attend, because the big surprise is no gift. Happy birthday, brother!

Consider your business. How do you handle mix-ups like mine? What if resolving service issues could be a gateway to expanding the relationship, revenues, and opportunities? There's a new way of looking at the same old challenges. You can be in the customer service business and the customer expansion business at the same time if you follow some important guidelines.

I learned more about these distinctions not when ordering wine, but when I got my first taste of Beer. Stafford Beer was one of the forefathers of modern management science. His life's work was based on cybernetics, a set of management principles that Beer developed and explored over the course of his lifetime.

In a nutshell, *cybernetics* is the science of how things are designed. Management cybernetics (a term coined by Beer) says that a system can only perform as it is designed. The whole idea behind his work was to allow people and leaders to construct systems that could adaptively perform in environments they could not fully control, such as the customer journey, for example.

He used an acronym POSIWID to clarify his work. POSIWID stands for the "purpose of a system is what it does." In other words, beyond good intentions, aspirations, and explanations, a system can only do what it is designed to do. Nothing more, nothing less.

Before you drink in more Beer, ask yourself this question: How is your customer experience system currently designed? Is your organization designed to serve the people in it so that the customer experience is expansive, leveraged, and maximized?

> **NOTE**
>
> *Customer Experience* (CX) is
> the overall impression you leave
> with your customer. Customer
> Experience is the very definition
> of your brand, your brand's value,
> and your opportunity for revenues.
> Multiple touch points factor
> into every customer experience,
> connecting sales, service, and
> customer success (as well as other
> departments) into every stage of
> the customer journey.

If the processes that power your customer experience are complex and overwrought, where is your purpose? Nobody wakes up and says, "Let's make our stuff difficult to access, hard to configure, and impossible to return." If you abdicate your responsibility because of third-party shipping, for example, you are giving up the ability to influence the process. Yet the experience—the journey—becomes as it is designed, if we don't inject a bit of genius into the operation.

- By definition, the customer journey is an environment that you cannot fully control, because it is dynamic.
- Nevertheless, even in a fluid environment, influence is never out of reach.
- Influence begins with listening—gaining a greater understanding of alternative points of view. Look for contradiction and corroboration, with a beginner's mindset, to uncover your genius.

Simplicity and ease are always available. Build them into the process. Ask your customers whether they see the changes as viable, valuable, and relevant. Then ask the genius question again: What could we do to make this easier for you?

Engage in the curiosity that's part of the beginner's mindset, and ask yourself—ask your customers—is that true? Look beyond belief to discover new ways of experience.

Now activate your beginner's mindset, as we tackle the "Seven Myths of Customer Experience."

The Seven Myths of Customer Experience

Myth #1: Customers demand quick answers and short call duration times.

Myth #2: The survey is the solution.

Myth #3: "Ease of Doing Business" is an operations play, so attacking it like a project is best.

Myth #4: Customer support is about resolving complaints.

Myth #5: We don't have the resources to transform our customer experience/customer support right now.

Myth #6: Great customer support is about agent knowledge, productivity, and extensive training.

Myth #7: The process is the solution.

At the intersection of complaints and possibilities, there is opportunity—an opportunity to step out of the overwhelm, rise above the noise, and simultaneously drive greater experience, engagement, and satisfaction.

Consider what my pal, Leslie, discovered when she helped customers to do their homework. She's the director of Market Strategy and Insights at a healthcare benefits company.

Leslie's team captured and reviewed numerous customer service center call recordings. They had conversations transcribed and then used tools to scan the transcriptions looking for key themes. "What we discovered," Leslie explains, "was that a high percentage of calls to the customer service center resulted in the agent giving the customer/member homework to 'go do.'"

Homework tasks ranged from getting documentation from their physicians and pharmacies to getting copies of test results and more. Scanning the transcriptions revealed that this was a key theme that customers commented on during the calls: "Why do you keep giving me homework assignments?" Those to-do items were a significant source of customer frustration.

Note that call times were short, and customers were not being put on hold. Also note that real solutions were not being provided. Callbacks went through the roof. Satisfaction went through the floor.

The solution? Various teams (customer service, market research, and executive leadership) reviewed the most frequent list of homework assignments given to customers. The teams chose three—just three!—that they could handle on the customers' behalf. Examples included asking the customer if they would be willing to hold while the customer service agent phoned the physician on the customer's behalf.

The alternative was the status quo: asking the customer to call the physician. Or call the provider. Or call both of them. And then call back to customer service. That's a lot of homework. Lots of opportunity for frustration. Lots of touchpoints that could impact customer perception. Yet Leslie's company had let go of the influence that was easily within their grasp. With no opportunity to assist or influence those steps on the customer journey, they were turning hope into a strategy—and leaving customers to fend for themselves. The customer journey was weeping with homework. There was only one way to dry the tears.

The company introduced the "No More Homework" initiative.

MYTH #1: CUSTOMERS DEMAND QUICK ANSWERS AND SHORT CALL DURATION TIMES

How did Leslie's team listen at a new level? It started with some surprising discoveries:

- Customers were willing to wait: Customers stayed on service calls longer when the reason to wait involved getting to resolution. Wouldn't you stay on the call if it meant getting what you wanted, without having to call back or to "do homework"? Leslie's customers felt the same way. A little bit of patience eliminated homework and escalated customer satisfaction.
- Customer service calls from "no homework" interactions revealed a significant percentage of customers commenting on the positive experience: Without explicitly being asked, customer service agents felt more motivated because they were able to solve customers' problems in real time. The hold times were acceptable, especially when compared with asking customers to call back (repeat callers can often be unpleasant, just as multiple callbacks lead to lower scores).

PS: I would have waited while Amy called the shipping company to find out the location of my brother's gift. That extra hold would have been time well spent. It might even have changed my Yelp! review. But I doubt it, because my brother's bottle of wine arrived three weeks after his birthday. Ouch! If you're curious how their customer service team is doing now, all I can tell you is: I don't know. I'm not their customer anymore.

MYTH #2: THE SURVEY IS THE SOLUTION

- How many surveys did Leslie's team send out before they discovered "too much homework" was really the problem? The answer is exactly zero, because what they discovered came from *actual listening*: transcripts of calls revealed what no survey ever could, because only the customers know what you really should be asking about—and then they ask you about it!

- Reducing reliance on surveys will put them in their place, namely you will see the survey as a useful (but often limited) tool.
- Surveys are not the solution because of two key flaws: (1) survey questions (even open-ended ones) rely on self-awareness and self-reporting. Often, customers just aren't aware of exactly "where it hurts." Yet the conversation always reveals what the survey won't. Because conversations are observed inside of a context that is most vital: the customer's context. (2) Since you initiate the questions, you drive the conversation. After all, it is your survey, right? In customer calls, the customer drives the agenda. They aren't answering your questions; rather, they are looking for their own answers. The drive and perspective inside customer calls will illustrate what no survey can: the customer's real issues, challenges, and desires.

MYTH #3: "EASE OF DOING BUSINESS" IS AN OPERATIONS PLAY, SO ATTACKING IT LIKE A PROJECT IS BEST

What would have happened if Leslie's company had said, "We need to come up with a project plan to address Ease of Doing Business (EODB) issues," and that initiative was assigned to a project team, perhaps in operations, or even a cross-functional team? Does this story sound familiar to you?

Companies do this all the time: They create a punch-list approach to resolving the critical issue of customer ease. Then, an individual or team is assigned the responsibility for handling all of the issues on the list.

When you identify issues and make them someone else's problem to solve, you lose accountability, effectiveness, and ownership.

EODB Is Not a Project, It's a Purpose

Believe in the myth of a portfolio solution, and here's what you'll discover:

- The project team has all of the responsibility and none of the authority.
- Ownership without influence does not work. This sounds like you just made "hope" a strategy.
- Status quo is maintained and observed instead of being modified quickly to serve the customer's best interests.
- Change happens at a snail's pace—if at all—because the people asked to manage the change aren't the ones who can truly enable it.

- Funding gets funky: An outside task force will struggle to get budget for even the best-laid plans because of competing internal priorities inside the portfolio.
- EODB isn't a punch list or an isolated responsibility. It's everyone's job, every day. Here's why:
  - Customer service experience is a key driver of overall loyalty. EVERY company wants loyalty. EVERY company would love to drive cost out of the customer service experience (and repeat calls are expensive).
  - For Leslie, every customer service employee knew exactly how to improve customer experience—"get rid of homework." Everyone was engaged, invested, and enrolled.
  - One person or one team didn't take on the responsibility for resolving an operational issue within the portfolio: the group mobilized quickly around an identified issue, and they resolved the "no homework challenge" as a group.
  - Building a "task force" and punch list would be creating internal homework, instead of resolving the problem as a team right away.
- What would you be willing to invest in order to gain greater loyalty, fewer callbacks, and greater satisfaction? A minor change for Leslie's company yielded major results!

The key was getting everyone inside Leslie's organization—from the leadership team to the front lines—listening to the voice of the customer. So they built a special booth to do it—an online web page where everyone could listen to customer comments—built around a monthly theme. The listening booth page showcases where the team is winning (and where they are not).

Go Beyond the Survey

Leslie's team sends a relationship survey to customers each year. At the end of each survey they include a question asking customers' permission to follow up for a live conversation after the survey concludes. The customer experience team then follows up with customers to conduct live, 10-minute interviews. The customer experience team randomly selects 15 percent of respondents for the follow-up conversation. Then they choose top executives to conduct those interviews.

In this program, the healthcare company's leaders hear feedback directly from customers on a variety of random topics. The key is that the topics and customers are not chosen or preselected by customer service (or anyone else). That way, there is no "ulterior motive" (for instance, using survey data to make an executive look bad, or only selecting happy customers so that the leader thinks that everything is rosy). This random approach means that executives listen with less ego because there's no agenda—only an opportunity to hear what's really going on.

MYTH #4: CUSTOMER SUPPORT IS ABOUT RESOLVING COMPLAINTS

Customer support is about *uncovering opportunities*. Please don't misunderstand: resolving complaints is important, but uncovering opportunities within those complaints is nothing short of genius.

Leslie has done her homework. The customer interview script starts with, "I'm here to listen to you and to advocate for you." Can you see the genius in that statement? How does that intro match up with how your service teams—or anyone else's—interacts with your customers? Language matters when it comes to customer connection. Start the conversation with service, and you teach people what matters most to your organization.

Keep resolving complaints, but don't just stop there. Keep looking and listening for opportunities. Customers will tell you what surveys never will, as Leslie has shared with me on more than one occasion!

Exec Listening Creates New Results

As a result of the customer interviews, Leslie's team discovered a new and underserved customer segment: customers who live on state borders. It seems that those boundaries created unexpected restrictions for some geographies.

Her company only has a presence in 14 states, members who live on state borders often choose nearby physicians in other states. Unknowingly, they are selecting out-of-network providers. These customers are hit with unexpectedly higher out-of-pocket costs, and the customer conversations reflected their dissatisfaction. On the state borders, scores were lower and customer service calls were higher. The company created programs targeted to improve education and satisfaction for this newly discovered customer segment.

Note once again that this information came through executive listening sessions. No survey was involved in this solution. Beneath the complaints, opportunity was discovered: Adjusting communication with customers on state borders reduced calls and increased customer satisfaction.

C-Sparks: If You Do Your Homework, Customers Won't Have To

What homework do you give your customers to do in order to resolve an issue? How could you make it easier for your customers to do business with you, simplifying their experience by managing one homework assignment on their behalf?

- Reinforce the top themes that matter to your customers and to your company. Prescribe actions that employees can take as a result of what they heard, and showcase examples where homework is eliminated or deeply reduced, so that employees identify (and internalize) best practices.
- The quality of customer feedback trumps the quantity of customer feedback. How could you bring the voice of your customer to every employee? Could you feature a recording in a Town Hall meeting, for example? Could it be a recording where a customer wasn't just singing your praises, but processing a real issue? Let's face it: Employees know the difference between PR and real solutions—don't be afraid to show the struggle. Otherwise, this sharing feels like a self-congratulating commercial, not an opportunity to learn. Choose a recording that can help you change service behavior, culture, and focus, sharing it with as many employees as possible.
- Invite customers from different geographies or industries to sit on a panel at your next company meeting. Ask questions of these customers—live in front of the Town Hall audience. Build live inquiry into the system!
- As evidence of Leslie's executive leadership, snippets from customer interviews, along with the interviewer name, are featured in the company's monthly newsletter. How could you select a customer and interviewer to highlight in your next Town Hall meeting or all-employee communication?
- What's the regular cadence or method you've developed for allowing every employee to hear the voice of the customer? Do you use newsletters? Internal web pages? Some other method? The only wrong answer is none of the above!

From Black Hole to Above Goal in 88 Days

When customers nickname your support experience "The Black Hole," what do you do?

Rapid expansion propelled a human capital software company to an inflection point. Multiple legacy systems, the result of acquisitions, weren't functioning as a cohesive unit. The message came in the form of multiple customer surveys: Fix your outdated systems or we are done. Transform or die.

The rigid legacy tiered support system, in which cases were created and then escalated, took too long and left customers unsatisfied. Have you been there?

The company developed a new collaborative model by which various departments and experts came together around a common goal: quick and unsiloed resolution to issues. They called the newly designed system "The Swarm."

Time-to-resolution affects customer satisfaction scores by as much as 40 percent or more, depending on your industry. For this Florida-based company, software changes meant that the Customer Success team received automated alerts when cases were not being resolved quickly. More than three hand-offs? That's evidence of silos, not a swarm. Alerts were sent and resources were rallied.

Armed with new information, the Customer Success teams knew exactly which actions to take to delight customers. The team set their sights on the final frontier: Case Avoidance. The best support experience, it's often said, is no support experience.

The Customer Success team implemented two solutions to help customers help themselves and each other. The first is a tool that indexes institutional knowledge and surfaces relevant content to customers proactively as they begin to log a case. The second was a corporate social network platform. Using the platform's collaboration features enabled Customer Success staffers—and even other customers—to answer questions in a customer-facing online group.

By shrugging off legacy tiered solutions and regrouping with a focus on speed, simplicity, and customer experience, the company transformed a black hole into a success story—one that brought value to both the customers and the company. The experience did more than solve a problem; it created a collaboration template for any company facing the challenge of change.

Along the way, the team developed a solution of manual hashtags to track cases and connect support team members. But the solution only worked if employees remembered to add the hashtags. When they forgot, which happened frequently, workload increased, and customer satisfaction decreased. Who would guide The Swarm and increase accountability? It turns out that it takes more than hashtags to really deliver a message.

Making adjustments quickly was the key to the company's success. Decision making was pushed down. The more employees felt empowered to do the right thing, the more they embraced the larger change strategy. The team, as a whole, took collective ownership. At first, it wasn't easy to see that the hashtags weren't working. By design, getting rid of an ineffective system happened quickly and easily (they swarmed it and it disappeared). When things weren't easy? The team reached out for new internal allies with experience and skills.

How well did the revamp work? Resolution time decreased nearly 20 percent, and 55 percent of Swarm requests received a response within 30 minutes—these were metrics that far exceeded the company's expectations. Judging from their satisfaction scores, The Swarm exceeded customer expectations as well, and pulled the company out of a black hole.

MYTH #5: WE DON'T HAVE THE RESOURCES TO TRANSFORM OUR CUSTOMER EXPERIENCE/CUSTOMER SUPPORT RIGHT NOW

How many new reps did the software company hire? What did they spend on training? Their genius didn't come from additional resources, but from the reconfiguration of existing ones. What resources do you have, right now, that can be repurposed for new results? Is it really a question of hiring new people, or of realigning the ones you have? For most organizations with whom I work, the focus is on the missing resources. It's a commonly held belief that you need more people to get better results. But this software company that swarmed got more from the people they already had when they designed the existing organization around their intended results. The cybernetics of The Swarm are a powerful lesson: You don't need to add people, time, or money to the system. Just line up the team that you have in a new way.

The results in Florida weren't the result of a five-year, five-phase, five-million-dollar investment. These results were produced inside of 90 days with no additional resources required. In fact, the customer-facing online resources leveraged a previously untapped expertise: namely, the expertise inside their customer base. Customers began solving one another's problems, augmenting the skill set of the company. Collaborating with their customers meant that they connected with untapped genius in an innovative new way. The Swarm pulled them out of the black hole, because that's what it was designed to do.

MYTH #6: GREAT CUSTOMER SUPPORT IS ABOUT AGENT KNOWLEDGE, PRODUCTIVITY, AND EXTENSIVE TRAINING

The Swarm was a design-based approach that built on *existing* training, expertise, and knowledge. As you know, solving customer issues is a team sport. If one person doesn't have the knowledge, he or she still has the resourcefulness to find someone who does. In The Swarm environment, those experts were coming forward and delivering their expertise. This software company has even explored peer-to-peer learning as a method of sharing knowledge across functions. Training is important, but finding solutions quickly is where genius comes to life. The Swarm has created a self-perpetuating pattern, built for expanding the customer base, not just serving it.

Make It Easier on Yourself

Kevin Hickey was perplexed. He was winning at the same time that he wasn't. Hickey found himself in this predicament when he was leading customer service for shipping giant Maersk in North America in 2018. At that time, he had 260 employees spread out across the U.S. and Canada, handling a business model that was so complex that he had key metrics going in opposite directions. How is that even possible?

The first step in the customer journey was making sure that the right customers were getting the right information, right on time. It's a shipping business, after all, with lots of on-the-ocean ships and other ways to move things around the globe. Maersk data showed that they were delivering the correct shipping details in 99 percent of customer engagements. However, the weekly volume of calls was spiking to over 800 inquiries. All of those calls focused on one issue: arrival information.

The global shipping business is a complicated beast. Hickey explains that there are "520 separate surcharges that can be applied to an invoice, including at least 25 variations on bunker (fuel) surcharges. And contracts can go through as many as 150 amendments a year. Rates themselves can change several times a week." Customers understand that variables are involved when shipping goods with Maersk; what they don't understand is when things happen and they don't know about it.

The big-picture initiative began with Maersk publishing its overall billing performance statistics. They discovered that the arrival notification process was being handled and counted differently in each of the four sites. The simple change of implementing a single best practice reduced the arrival query volume by 40 percent in just four weeks.

C-Sparks: The Value of Consistency

Great experiences result from processes perfected over time.

Does your business count things differently in different locations? Why?

- Whether it's a tool, a process, or a procedure, look for clues about which method contributes to timely resolution and consistent customer experience. Then be consistent in how you engage other functions in your company that contribute to customer support and experience. If that is finance for improving a return, use the same process or tool for every finance person or team that you engage. It bears repeating: Great experiences result from processes perfected over time. That pursuit of perfection must be consistent!

- When employees develop workarounds and one-offs (hacks), it's either because the process is broken or because they found an easier way. What are the hacks and workarounds that are happening right now in your organization? Instead of getting upset about processes that aren't being followed, get something else.
- Get curious. Coloring outside of the lines is drawing a picture of what processes are incomplete. Or broken. If employees are finding new ways of doing things, it's not a sinister plot, mutiny, or organized defiance. It's an indication of what you need to fix. The outlier team might be showing you a new set of rules and possibilities. Design your process for curiosity, consistency, and observation. Drive the details that matter, explained in ways that everyone from Detroit to Denmark can understand.

There is a way to do it better. Find it.
Thomas Edison, Inventor of the Electric Light Bulb

"We needed that sort of early win," Kevin explains, "to show people that the process could be effective. Before that, we were getting feedback saying that there wasn't time to do all this analysis because there were so many fires to fight. Just doing some basic analysis showed they would have a lot fewer fires to fight." Year to date, the teams have reduced overall email inquiries by 26 percent.

Today, a performance scorecard is issued, not by the customer, but by the vendor—Maersk itself. Kevin says that some of his more sophisticated customers have their own scorecards for Maersk, but whichever way the conversation is driven, it is based on data. That basis, Kevin says, has removed a lot of the hostility and back-and-forth that used to occur. "It's much more of a partnership now, because the data will sometimes point to inefficiencies on the customer side, and it will help them in that way, too." Kevin says they are piloting a "joint scorecard" with some of their larger (big box retail) customers, "where we both have skin in the game for the betterment of the partnership."

Make success as easy to see as a Jumbotron. That way, everyone sees the same definition—that joint scorecard that lets you know whether you're winning. Or not.

MYTH #7: THE PROCESS IS THE SOLUTION

Too much beer isn't good for you.

System design, particularly around the customer experience, is vital to any company's success. But remember, a system is another example of a tool. What makes any tool useful? The people who use it.

Building the fastest Formula One racecar in the world is an engineering feat of incredible potential. But without a driver, pit crew, and other people, the machine can't perform. "We've invested in speedy systems," your management team might say. But that's not the whole story, because people bring the process to life.

When it comes to success, the whole is greater than the sum of its parts. You have your divisions, silos, customers, and teams. But together, working toward a single goal, a team of teams is what makes the system work. That's what Maersk discovered: unified, consistent processes were the result of managing a team of teams. Hickey and friends uncovered a myth-busting maxim: If excellence ceases to exist in one part of the organization, by definition, excellence ceases to exist.

The challenge for leaders in customer experience is to see that everyone—every team—has to win. Together, you are fighting for your customers. The internal battle is for consistency, from sales to service delivery to support. Alignment is the name of the game. Are you designing your process around an adaptable model that leverages all of your resources?

Great experiences result from processes perfected over time. Until you are able to fix the problems of today consistently, customers won't explore where you have the potential to go. But genius is revealed when service provides solutions in a context of listening, exploring, and seeking.

Ask the right questions of your teams, and you'll discover how to build the solutions that your customers crave. Ignore those cravings, and it doesn't matter what your team of brilliant minds have brainstormed on conference room walls. That well-thought-out whiteboard journey is always incomplete, no matter how smart the authors might be, without the central character in the story—the customer. In the next chapter, we'll expand on several innovative ideas to help you capture the real story. To listen more effectively. To break free from old patterns.

As you scan the horizon of your customer journey, there's still something that's blocking your path. We've talked about asking the right questions. You've observed companies that aren't afraid to break through myths and misunderstandings. But there's one thing that's still out there derailing your best efforts, obstructing your achievement, and impairing your results.

Do you know what it is?

CHAPTER 10

The Secret Sauce

An intriguing message showed up in my LinkedIn mailbox:

"Hi Karen, I'm in an executive development program and my focus is on CSAT and loyalty. I consider you a leading expert in the field of Customer Satisfaction. I've got a great opportunity in front of me, but I could use some help. Would you be open to the connection?"

One click later, I met Tara. Her background was impressive. Her email exchange revealed that she was engaged in an overhaul of her company's VoC (Voice of the Customer) program, reducing barriers to transformation and several other meaty challenges. She wanted guidance on an important presentation that had just taken place. It hadn't gone as planned, and she wanted my help to understand why.

Tara was clearly a rising star on a mission: Her CEO wanted to reduce barriers to change. Or so he said. The audience was the President's Council: global company leaders responsible for multiple divisions and key products across a worldwide organization. It was a career opportunity, wrapped in a PowerPoint.

"Hi everybody, I'm so glad you're here." The millennial superstar took the floor and started her pitch. Some faces in the room were familiar, most were not. Her slides were colorful, but not too colorful—a combination of pie graphs, statistics, and bar charts that reflected deep research and listening. The leaders sat silent. The payoff came on a single slide: a comparison of the top five and bottom five products, based on customer satisfaction scores and surveys. Revenues were correlated, projections were provided, the data told the story. "Thank you," she said in conclusion, knowing she nailed it.

Instead of boardroom banter, the response was more like a barroom brawl.

The executives began by throwing punches at each other. Protests erupted from the execs whose products showed up in the bottom five, confronting the "lucky ones" who had received better CSAT (customer satisfaction) scores. "Lucky" because the data was incomplete, the European division leader said, as she slammed the lid on her laptop.

What started as a multinational global conflict shifted into a united front. United against data. United against the scores. United against . . . Tara.

The guy from Boston said she didn't talk to enough customers. Another accused her of not talking to enough influencers. Still one more questioned the methodology: Tara had double-majored in marketing and philosophy. Did she really have the chops to dive deep into these statistics?

Tara was the messenger.

Tara was the target.

Tara was in trouble.

"Tara, no prospects were included," the senior leader from Asia said, turning to the CEO and speaking in a fast-paced, staccato style. "I mean, she didn't even take into account the fact that we could be talking to customers and getting new customers, because, well, it's easy to see. Just think about it. Look at new sales. Sales would solve our market share issue, making these satisfaction scores a moot point. What about our new product, the Prestidigi-tator? Satisfaction around low-performing products isn't really going to build our revenues for the next year! That's not our strategy. Our new products, like the Prestidigitator, are the future. And that future isn't even in any of these slides." He threw down his pen in disgust.

The CEO leaned in and spoke for the first time. "Well, what are we going to do?"

"Actually," Tara offered in a calming tone, undeterred by hearing the pen drop, "we went in to talk to customers about this product—this Prestidigita-tor. When we shared that we had something new and we described it, a vast majority said, 'We don't really see that as a viable product.' Here's the graph of the results." Appendix Slide I was on the screen. The label, written in Hel-vetica at the top, said "Viability."

"On follow-up, nearly two-thirds said, 'We probably wouldn't buy a prod-uct like that from you,'" she continued, clicking over to the next slide, which was labeled "Sourcing." "Our customers just don't see us as a viable provider for this solution." She paused for a split second, trying to shift the conversa-tion in a new direction. "There's a major market inflection point here in the data, if you want to . . ."

No one heard what she said next. The exact percentages from "Viability" and "Sourcing" had stopped everyone in their tracks.

Then they started up again: "The description of the product was wrong!" "The survey was incomplete!" "Tara, did your team share the latest marketing specifications or a prior version?"

Tara was excused from the meeting before she could really satisfy the inquisition.

Disrupted and disturbed, the executives did everything except listen. Instead of taking in vital information, they became united in attacking a common enemy: Tara. Overcome by a desire to defend their products, positions, and divisions, they missed the message.

They shot the messenger.

Have you ever been there?

Tara was blindsided and confused. She told the story that the data revealed; what had she done wrong? In one-on-one meetings with some of the leadership team, there were no issues. (Taking individual meetings with several key leaders, Tara had done her prep work—or so she believed.) Suddenly the numbers—the same numbers that she shared in private conversations—were intolerable. Unacceptable. Impossible.

Why?

Because data, statistics, and numbers are no match for executive ego.

Shortly after the presentation, the CEO made a "Captain's Call," as Tara explained it to me. A colleague who had just moved into marketing was now responsible for VoC. Tara was moved casually from high potential to high risk after just one meeting. The company had "reallocated her responsibilities." The move happened without consulting Tara's boss, but her boss didn't want to fight it.

The Prestidigitator failed to meet expectations. The company began losing market share, profitability, and customers—but not as a result of Tara's reassignment. Ignoring her advice had caused all the problems.

The company adopted a policy that the satisfaction scores were really a marketing issue: better and more frequent messaging would resolve the customer perception challenges, as well as boost sales numbers.

The company was going to sell itself to satisfaction. Products were going to be produced and offered, because more products for more people was the way to profitability . . . or so they thought.

Unfortunately, their customers didn't agree. They didn't have a voice in the conversation, so they voted with their wallets. And their feet. They walked away and spent money with the competition.

Was Tara upset by these changes? No. With my help, she made some changes of her own. She was very happy in her new role at another company. Today, she still gives great presentations—filled with honesty and authenticity—at an organization where people are willing and able to hear what she has to say.

WHAT HAPPENS WHEN EGO ENTERS THE CONVERSATION

Defensiveness can be destructive when data is seen as a weapon. For Tara, even the leaders who had nodded in agreement at her findings (prior to the meeting) started blamestorming when the CEO was in the audience. They blamed the data. They blamed the team that gathered the data. They blamed the person who delivered the data.

When people feel threatened, even unintentionally, it's impossible to hear the feedback above the fear.

If the purpose of feedback in your organization is to put people on trial for the bottom five products while you celebrate the fortunate ones on top, how's that working for you? Or for them? What happens if leadership steps back and considers the following:

> The purpose of customer feedback is to help reimagine a future that's more successful, with greater retention, sales, and loyalty. So what if, instead of looking for winners and losers, we start looking for possibilities and (process) problems?

If your customer feedback is presented once a quarter, or twice a year at the President's Council, you're going to be managing a dynamic business based on static results. A single point of reporting to reflect an ever-changing customer landscape: Does that look like a genius system design to you?

In an annual or semiannual model, customer feedback ignites ego like a match instead of bringing in a fire extinguisher. Static stats can oversimplify results, drive defensiveness, and burn through resources that could be pointed in another, more valuable direction.

But that direction can only be discovered when you take ego out of the conversation.

WHAT'S NECESSARY ISN'T ALWAYS EASY

I felt for Tara because I've been Tara. I've been the messenger. Maybe you have, too.

I've been the object of massive objections. I've been in a joint presentation where the other guy got shot and dismissed. I got to stay, sitting in the room while I wished for an invisibility cloak, listening to the leadership team tear this guy apart. It wasn't pretty. More importantly, it wasn't useful.

Defensiveness and ego are the enemy of good listening. It's one thing to listen to the voice of the customer, but until you can share that information with the people who need to hear it, your work is incomplete.

Today, I invite you to continue your listening journey. Whether you are an executive or someone who shares customer insights, it's time to hear things in new ways. I want messengers to survive and thrive, without ego derailing the story that needs to be heard. For C-Suite leaders, my message is on the masthead. I say this gently, but firmly: Listen Up!

There is a way to do what's necessary, even for the toughest audience.

No matter how strong your questions, data, and systems design, your success depends on one vital element. I call it the Secret Sauce: taking ego out of the conversation.

That's what AuthentiCx (http://authenticx.com) does for their customers. They find the data that really matters, and they deliver it in a way that cannot be denied.

"Most companies hire us to tell them who they need to fire," Amy Brown says, stirring a cappuccino. She pushes a fistful of brown curls over her right ear, revealing tiny turquoise earrings that match her eye color exactly. "Customer data reflects your customer's experience. Sometimes leaders aren't ready to look in the mirror."

Brown is the founder and CEO of AuthentiCx. Her company specializes in gathering feedback and providing easy-to-access information that summarizes customer conversations. "Our platform helps execs to make sense out of what is driving customer behavior, how to categorize it, and what to do about it." Here's how ego comes into the picture for Amy, and how she erases it.

"For most companies, customer service interactions fall in the category of 'store and ignore,'" she shares, pointing at her tablet where a 3-D chart is brightly displayed. "Every leader says that they're data-driven and that the numbers matter. We always have data presented visually so leaders can see how big a problem is and how prevalent. But we also help them to understand what it feels like from a customer's perspective."

What's more powerful than a pie graph? "The literal voice of the customer has so much more impact. Behind closed doors, executives will tell me, 'I feel so distanced from our customers.' That's why we play audio files for them, so they can hear customer feedback straight from the source."

Without a survey to filter it, the voice of the customer becomes difficult to ignore.

"One CFO told me he wanted to puke after hearing the experience his customers were having." Amy shakes her head at the image. How do other leaders react to hearing the voice of the customer? "The glasses come off the head. People push back from the table. There are sighs. Even tears welling up in the eyes."

When leaders access that stream of authentic feedback for the first time, is it like putting your toe in icy water? "More like diving into a freezing river, headfirst," Amy says.

"Audio is more powerful than the data itself. Every day, in unsolicited conversations, your customers are telling you what they think, what disappoints them, and what they wish you had."

For her C-Suite clients, Brown plays a montage of customer service calls that reflect the data. By providing curated, categorized conversations to the CEOs she serves, she helps companies avoid what she calls "eddies." She's not talking about Redmayne or Van Halen; she's talking about the things that cause the currents to change in a rushing river or stream.

These eddies, she explains, are typically caused by boulders or some other obstacle—the kind of object that creates a swirling and unexpected flow inside of a fast-moving river. Imagine your customers in a raft, their journey moving downstream with predictable speed. When the current swirls and shifts, pulling the raft toward the rocks, the fun stops. Disaster can strike quickly.

These barriers and eddies are part of the customer journey. Listening for customer obstacles is the first step in avoiding them. Hearing those concerns and questions directly from recorded calls can help take ego out of the conversation.

C-Sparks: Ready to Shred the Survey?

What Matters Most in the Conversation

The limitation of survey data is that it's one-directional. You can't ask follow-up questions. You can't have interactions. With recorded conversations, senior execs can listen in at any time of the day or night. What's your plan to share that story, or those stories, with senior leaders? Recordings mean that you don't need a messenger—curate the content and support the dialogue with data. How will you provide clear and ongoing access to the feedback that matters—not just prerecorded praise calls (which do nothing to help avoid eddies along the journey)? If the customer delivers the message, you can't mess with the messenger!

Orchestrate "Aha!" moments privately

If you discover information that could ultimately impact a particular executive leader, share it privately before you share it publicly! While Tara shared some details, she didn't touch base with everyone prior to the meeting. Nobody likes being "called on the carpet," especially when their performance is tied to your data.

Keep Off the Carpet

Gain some agreement about the goals for the meeting. Get really clear on the agenda . . . and the hidden agendas. One of the things that Tara discovered was that she had been sent on a "science experiment" for the Prestidigitator. More than one executive was betting the future on this new product; the customer feedback had to support that investment, or it was going to be a real problem (and it was). Of course, none of the senior leaders gave her that context. Instead of listening to valuable input, leaders were gambling their future on an uncertain product that the listening didn't support. Then they doubled down and bet against Tara's insights.

A treacherous aspect of ego is that it makes people withhold information and context. Without that context, the messenger flusters and fails. Don't let this scenario happen to you. Ask wise questions of your leadership team: without understanding the implications, it's nearly impossible to deliver data in a way that sidesteps the egos in the room. What's at stake for them? What results are they hoping that the surveys/numbers/listening reveals? What's the outcome they're most afraid to hear? Find out their context, and you won't get called onto the carpet.

Next-level influence is how listening turns into action, as Russell Wilson (http://linkedin.com/in/russwilson) learned. At Google, he built and scaled one of the largest UX (user experience) organizations within the company. As part of his research, he created and distributed a survey to his peers outside of Google, at widely diverse organizations. Here's what he discovered:

- We don't work with endusers enough.
- We don't always work on the right things (even when we think we are doing so).
- We don't think like business owners.

These data points earned him an exclusive seat at the next executive briefing, joining the agenda of a very senior leader. He outlined his observations, data points, and expectations, thinking that he crushed it. Soon, the next meeting agenda comes out and, to his surprise, his time had been allocated to some of his peers. Eventually, as further agendas were developed, he was moved into more of an observational (nonspeaking) role in the meetings. What happened?

"I was talking in the language of a practitioner," he explains from his current office at Fidelity in Boston, where he now serves as the Chief Design Officer. "Three bullet points got me into the room. Overloading the story with details and design-speak was what limited my impact. What I was saying was vitally important, but the way I was saying it meant no executive was able to hear it."

"That's not uncommon," according to Chris Westfall, author of *Leadership Language: Using Authentic Communication to Drive Results* (Wiley, 2018). Westfall has provided communications guidance to companies like Experian, Unilever, HP, and Discover, and he's coached clients onto *Shark Tank, Dragons Den* in Canada, and *Shark Tank Australia*. "They say 'the devil's in the details' because, when it comes to the C-Suite, those details can drag you straight to hell. The challenge is: We all speak the same language, but we don't understand what the story is really about."

He goes on to explain that it's not about denying the details, but you have to consider something called "point of attack." From a narrative or storytelling standpoint, point of attack simply means where the narrative begins. The strongest stories start with action, and chronological order can be a long and winding road to your destination. Coming straight at the thing that matters is something that most people rarely do, but that's what C-Suite leaders really need.

"What do executives care about?" he asks, coming straight at the thing that matters. "Outcomes. Implications. Results. Here's a principle of effective communication: The strongest message starts with what your listener is thinking. In my book, I talk about how I was working with a coaching client in Eastern Europe. This guy was amazing—he spoke five languages. So I ask him a stupid question: 'Erik, why are we speaking English today?' The answer is simple: 'because it's the only language you understand.'"

Rather than begin with your own viewpoint, the best communication strategy actually starts with what's top of mind for the executive of your choice. Speaking their language is the way to earn a seat at the table, because it establishes relevance. And resonance: You show that even though you may not agree with their objectives, you see them. You understand their agenda. By understanding other perspectives, your opportunity for sharing becomes clear.

Westfall explains it like this, "Karen, you do a lot of keynotes, just like me, and there's one thing I've learned. Start with your audience and you'll never go wrong. It's counterintuitive," he continues, "and you may not believe this, but I fell out of love with my own material a long time ago. Creating results is the reason for the conversation. If I don't meet an audience where they are—really connecting with them—will anyone care what's on slide 47? No. But when you talk about what really matters to people, they can't help but listen.

"We are taught to make our arguments then draw to a conclusion but focusing on outcomes first—for the C-Suite—is where the conversation begins, not with describing how you do your job or the nuances of the intricacies of the data you've mined."

C-Sparks: Pro Tip—Pump Up the Preso in One Slide

Here's how to emphasize results and connect with a C-Suite audience in your next preso (presentation):

1. Replace the agenda slide with a slide called "Outcomes."
2. Ask the leaders in the room to review your list. Where would they like to dive deeper first? I'd rather talk about what's top of mind for the audience instead of being married to a well-thought-out agenda. How about you? If you've built the presentation, are you going to lose your mind if someone asks you to start on slide number 7? I hope not! Besides, in some circles, that agenda slide just helps people plan when they can check out and check their phones.
3. Start by talking about what matters most to your audience, instead of trying to make them fall in love with the order of your slides.
4. *Pro Tip:* nobody really cares about the agenda! You have a certain amount of time, it's usually scarce, so find the "point of attack" that serves the room (not your agenda) best. If someone says, "We're really pressed for time, your 15 minutes is now five," you're ready. That's not a problem when you have everything you want to say on your "Outcomes" slide!

But what about the desire to dive into the details? "I work with thousands of entrepreneurs; many are engineers, scientists, and inventors," Westfall says. "As you might expect, they want to describe how the widget functions, the scientific history behind the medical device, or what happens on line 497 of the code. Important stuff! That's how things work, and without that focus the business doesn't exist. I get it. But how you drive your business is different from how you *describe* your business. When I tell a detail-oriented entrepreneur that no one cares how they make the sausage, I try to do it gently. Then I ask a question: Would you like to know what really matters? If they say, 'yes,' I say, 'outcomes.' A question from the C-Suite about how anything works is really a question of *how can you make this thing work for me*, or by extension, *for our organization?*

"Look in the direction of impact, because that's where your leaders are looking: They want to know the implications. Words like 'so that' and 'because' force us to look in the direction of service," he explains, reinforcing the concept of servant leadership.

"If you are trying to educate your executive team, stop. Do they need to be smarter? Maybe. But is it your job to teach them?" he shakes his head, pointing out that he shares more in this video (https://bit.ly/listenup-chriswestfall). "You don't have to prove how smart you are, how well educated you are, or how much of an SME [subject-matter expert] you are in order to help people." There's something more important than your methodology, credibility, or even your IQ, according to Chris.

"Insight starts the conversation. I've heard you say it before, Karen. You call it 'actionable insights,' right? Those kinds of insights will earn you a seat at the table. Instead of talking about how hard you and your team worked to prepare the presentation, shift to a higher gear. Instead of discussing your experience, convey it, demonstrate it, and own it in the way you approach the conversation. You use language to show how you see the viewpoint—the puts and takes—of the leadership team." He stops and takes a breath. "Just keep the TLAs out of the conversation."

Would that be a "three-letter-acronym"?

"Correct," he deadpans.

A great way to know that you're not speaking the language of leadership is when executives say things like, "Yes, thanks, wow, uh-huh, yep, this is great. I'm not sure what you want me to do with this information, but this has been a great update. Nice work." You feel good, but nothing happens.

Nodding is not always acceptance, action, or agreement.

"Praise doesn't feed the bulldog," Westfall chimes in. "There are two types of language, really," Chris continues. "Creation and observation. Creation language is the language of agreement, teamwork, action items, and goals. Observation language is, well, observation: reports, news, data, praise, and descriptions. We need both in order to be clear about anything of real importance. But which kind of language matters most in the executive office?" Notice when you're sharing the news in observation mode, and what happens when you shift to creation mode. Where do you find traction, connection, action, and impact?

"Execs are interested in creating something: new revenues, new results, new shareholder value," Westfall tells me via video call from his home office in Houston. "Leadership language is selective by nature: Choose the words that will help you most when you want to connect with the C-Suite. See what you can create, in terms of real value, for the leaders you wish to influence."

C-Sparks: Karen's Secret Sauce—Take Ego Out of the Conversation

Why is it that some organizations (executives) are effective at leveraging feedback to create a unifying, rallying cry to connect and inspire their teams to a higher sense of purpose? Meanwhile, others are left staring at the scoreboard, tallying up winners and losers, pointing fingers, and deciding whom to blame. More often than not, ego takes over and results suffer because of it. True leaders know that they need the courage to hear the truth, and they need team members who aren't afraid to tell it, using leadership language. Are you ready to find out how to look in the direction of impact and outcomes? Here's the secret sauce:

Step Out of the Silos

When feedback is solicited in silos, readouts exist in silos and there's a siloed viewpoint on how to take action. In the next chapter, we'll talk about how setting up silos creates conflict, not cooperation. But for now, break down barriers by looking at key themes. Listen for these themes across segments, geographies, and distribution channels. If your questions are designed around a company function, you're not functioning as a cohesive team. Ego will enter the conversation, as executives defend their territory. What are the themes and ideas that matter to the entire organization? Look upstream: Examine big impact questions, genius questions, questions that shatter myths, and you're looking in the right direction.

Go Horizontal Instead of Vertical

Look for commonalities and trends in the top five/bottom five exercise. Go beyond stack ranking: Are there patterns that point to potential threats or opportunities? What's the interrelationship between all of the feedback at the bottom and at the top? In a context of common goals, look for common interests.

Privatize the Conversation

There can be no "aha!" moments in public, unless you've shared them in private. Period. Before a high-stakes meeting, where your message could start a fire around someone's ego, extinguish it before it starts. Share data and get curious: What do these numbers mean to the executive right in

(continued)

(continued)

front of you? Share what you see as the potential implications and look for agreement, or a challenge, before you are grilled in the boardroom. Someone's challenge may not change the numbers—or the way you present them—but you'd better be sensitive to the puts and takes in the room before you strike a match.

Serve Before You Speak

In your one-on-one, ask the genius question that you already know: How could I make this easier for you? You can't change results, hide information, or soft-pedal the truth. You're not there to play Santa Claus or grant wishes. But given what we know now, doesn't it make sense to talk about a potential solution, especially with the leader who cares most about it? If you're going to say, "Well, I'm a marketer, I can't help" you're giving up your power, inviting ego into the conversation, and minimizing your impact. You want a seat at the table? Step up and serve powerfully. You might be invited to sit down if you look in the direction of solutions, not just statistics. Maybe there's nothing that you can do right now except to listen. So do it! Why not do what you do best? You will be better informed in helping to craft a solution. In an earlier chapter, I asked: Are you in the customer service business or the customer expansion business? Now, here's a follow-up: Isn't that executive your customer, too? I hope so. Look in the direction of service, and you can reframe readouts. Bad news followed by a good solution is a soft place to land.

Shift Focus, Take It One Step at a Time

Ask forward-facing questions of your exec: What do you see as our best path forward? How will we know when this problem is solved? What's the first step you hope we take following this meeting? How can we leverage a team, or a team of teams, to accelerate results? Remember, a little bit of feedback is easier to take than a lot. A small fire is easily extinguished, but if the entire warehouse is burning . . . well, you get the idea. The message here is: stay in touch, connect frequently, and share data in a way that makes your insights easier to handle. (In my experience, video and telephone calls work better than email!)

Let Customers Share Their Stories

Bring the voice of the customer into the one-on-one and into the boardroom. Create a regular cadence (not twice a year!) where customer feedback is shared consistently. Get out of the QBR (quarterly business review) mentality: Go at the pace of the business, rather than the pace of the survey. That way, you are regularly connecting in real time to the people who matter most (your customers and your executive team).

Watch Out for Eddies

How can you gain agreement that looking for swirling eddies is everyone's job? What are you doing right now to open up lines of communication between the front lines and the C-Suite? At USAA, they encourage innovation through their "Always On Ideas" platform, a portal that's available to all employees (https://bit.ly/listenup-usaa). They recently recognized the one, single employee who came up with the most patents—25 in total. Guess who did it? The security guard working the front gate! That's right, the ideas submitted helped to improve a key portion of the USAA customer experience. Anyone can innovate, if you're willing to listen. How can you create a forum where innovation can thrive? How do your C-Suite leaders hear how employees are accessing new insights? Listen and curate content that shares that impact. Analysis isn't enough: taking ego out of the conversation means injecting value and insight into it.

But how does listening work, exactly, in times of chaos, uncertainty, and unprecedented competition? In the next chapter, we will look at how listening is the best way—and in many cases the only way—to survive and thrive. We'll look at a story of a certain coach who put together an unlikely team and conquered an unbeatable foe. Because, along his journey, he learned how to make his own miracles. Not by turning water into wine, but by understanding what it takes to deal with disruption. Following that, we'll take a look at the steps that you can take right now to bring what we've discussed so far into a new kind of context where customer listening takes center stage.

CHAPTER 11

Dealing with Disruption

There will always be, forevermore, for the rest of time, and for all eternity, huge disruptors.

- Your competition comes up with a new product.
- An unexpected and highly aggressive competitor enters your market.
- Regulations change dramatically.
- There's a major world event, and it impacts everyone's life and business model.

I think you know what I mean.

In times of turmoil, whether that's 9/11, a global financial crisis, or the coronavirus pandemic, businesses are trying to think about how they can get back to growth. And leaders are looking for partners who can help them get there.

When disruption pushes the reset button on your relationships with your customers, you may be wondering: What does success look like now? As Marshall Goldsmith said, "What got you here won't get you there."

If there's one thing we've learned, dealing with the upheaval of recent world events, it's that adaptability and agility aren't just ideas. These concepts are the foundation of any business that's going to survive and thrive in the midst of disruption.

The companies that cross the chasm and make it into the Age of the Customer are the ones that innovate beyond their circumstances.

What's the secret for dealing with disruption? Listening more, not less.

There are three questions—three Catalyst Questions—that every company can ask customers when they are dealing with disruption:

- How can I help you right now?
- What does success look like for you on the other side of this?
- How can we build your return-to-growth plan together?

These Catalyst Questions are vital during times of disruption. Approaching the conversation with compassion, concern, and commitment can help your customers to see hidden possibilities. When you are in the middle of the tornado, it's hard to see that you actually might come through this—or just how you might survive. Have you been there?

A very important customer was about to go through a renewal. The contract at stake was a large piece of business. Big business means big attention to detail in my world.

So I did what I thought were all the right things. I followed the rules.

I asked questions about any obstacles that might be standing in our way. I discovered that there were lots of legal issues during the last contract negotiation. In fact, my senior VP contact at the customer told me horror stories of an almost-year-long process of back and forth between attorneys.

Well, I wanted to make the process as easy as possible.

I had done my behind-the-scenes work to get my boss's boss's boss (that's not a typo—there were a lot of links in the chain) to commit to a special request.

I asked him if he would fly from the New Jersey headquarters to Louisville, Kentucky, and sit in a conference room until the contract was resolved. We thought that this level of commitment would be fantastic, an unprecedented show of support and talent that would resolve any issues in person and in short order. Together, we would deliver the details in a consolidated show of force, in the customer's office, and would establish our unwavering commitment to resolving any contract issues.

But part of dealing with disruptions is understanding that plans don't always go as planned.

Encouraged by the response from headquarters, I asked that skip-two-levels VP to fly into Indianapolis, not Louisville. Together, we could take a two-hour drive down I-65 to the customer's office. We would meet with the customer, delivering the good news of the single resource that would make this big contract a done deal. The senior executive said yes, and it sounded like pure genius to me.

I'm not really a car person, but the blue Lexus rental car that pulled up to my office was a stunner. Long and sleek and loaded with leather, that chariot made a strong impression as I opened the door. I sunk into the passenger seat next to Mike, the aforementioned Senior Executive, and we began our journey.

I was feeling a combination of comfort and anxiety. Both feelings stayed with me as we made small talk between the cornfields of Southern Indiana, headed across the Ohio River to the big meeting.

We walked into the comfortable lobby and clicked our way across the shining marble floor to the front desk. I saw the receptionist, but I was picturing victory in my mind. She was a cheerful, thin woman in her midforties, with her hair pulled back in a bun. We approached and I let her know who we were there to see. She asked about the purpose of our meeting and we exchanged pleasantries. She dialed the executive office; we took five steps back toward the door and sat down in the waiting area.

A long, three-seat Barcelona sofa was our resting place. Armless, it was a couch that looked better than it felt. In front of us, an elaborate red rug covered a marble floor, marking off a space for visitors to sit. Separating the chairs and sofa, a square glass coffee table hosted an enormous display of white and purple orchids. Behind us, an elaborate cappuccino machine decorated a nearby granite countertop.

At this moment in time, as you might guess, I didn't need any caffeine.

I was doing one last round of meeting prep with the Senior Vice President, running through some Q&A scenarios. He sat facing me on my right, his back to the receptionist. Over his shoulder, I had a clear line of sight to the high desk just a few steps away. I saw that the receptionist was still on the phone. That was curious.

She gently put down the phone and turned to look at us. The smile on her face had been replaced with a straight line. My heartbeat started to increase, and I wasn't sure why.

My traveling companion, the Senior VP, couldn't see what I was beginning to suspect.

"Unfortunately," the receptionist said, "Tim is unavailable. He's not able to meet with you."

Now my heart started racing. My breathing got real shallow, real quick. I could feel the blood flush in my ears.

What?!?

I had confirmed the meeting earlier in the day, via email. We were standing right here. We had just driven two hours. We had what they needed . . . and they were saying no?

How could this be happening?

The receptionist was saying that he was in the building, but he was not going to be able to meet with us today. "You'll have to come back," she said with an obligatory smile that vanished in the same moment it had appeared.

No real excuse.

No real explanation.

No real luck.

I looked at the Senior VP. I looked at her. I couldn't even respond.

I hung my head in a combination of shame and horror.

I just knew Mike was going to look at me and lose his mind. He did not speak. We walked back to the car in silence. The Lexus that looked like a chariot on the way down started to look like a prison cell. His eyes straight ahead, Mike's stoic expression told me everything I needed to know—words were unnecessary. I was positive about what was going to happen next.

I was about to get fired.

Mike closed the car door and took a deep breath.

His thick fingers wrapped around the steering wheel for support. Or maybe to contain his rage? He'd played football and was an imposing presence. His broad shoulders borrowed from every inch of the Lexus's leather seat. He turned to look at me for the first time since we left the receptionist's desk.

"Are you under the impression I'm going to fire you right now?" he asked.

"Yes," I replied.

I was looking at the blank navigation screen in the center console, not at him. The parking lot was nearly empty. I held a bright blue pen in my hand, as if I were getting ready to open my notebook and write down his response.

He laughed.

"Here's the thing," he said, as I found the courage to face him. "This happens to all of us. There are moments when things are unexpected. So here's what we're going to do," he explained as he started the car. "We're going to go grab some dinner and we're going to get to know each other a little bit better. This is done, at least for today. We're going to take a pause. But here we are." The engine purred to life and he touched a button to put the car in gear. "Let's figure out how I can help you, right now."

I breathed a sigh of relief that seemed to last until the third quarter of the following year.

What felt like incredible disruption to me and my career is nothing compared to the disruption that your customers feel in times of uncertainty and change. My story pales in comparison, but the disorientation, fear, and confusion are common threads for all of us.

What helped me to keep from going quietly insane was Mike's simple cure for unexpected circumstances: ***Compassion***.

In times of turmoil, understanding is the antidote.

The only real mistake is the one from which we learn nothing.

Henry Ford

When you reach out and ask, "How can I help you right now?" that compassion can be met with the depth of response that brings opportunity to uncertainty.

When I went to dinner with my Senior Vice President, he asked me some questions about what things would be like on the other side of that contract negotiation and how he could help bring the resources to bear. I needed to be in that conversation so that we could figure out how to change our situation. At times of deep crisis, your customers need your compassion—and your ability to listen—more than ever. We looked past the pain of our circumstances and then, only then, were we able to see some alternatives. Together, we began to build a return to growth plan. It was a journey that never could have started without compassion and understanding in a time of crisis.

> In the end, everything is going to be ok. And if it's not ok, it's not the end.
>
> *John Lennon*

A NEW DESTINATION

I was reminded that no moment lasts forever. Although I had just made what felt like a horrible mistake, disrupting a very busy guy and burning up an entire afternoon for exactly no outcome, there was still something left to discover. I had to abandon my preconceptions in order to see it. I had to pause and let go of what I thought was going to happen to see where I really was.

Agreements go south. Deals don't get done. Disruption happens. These are the facts of life and business, reinforced during times of disarray in an unpredictable market.

Mike understood the power of compassion at a time of chaos.

Although we were traveling together, he arrived at a certain destination long before I did. He arrived at acceptance. What can you do, right now, to accept where you are—where your customers are—instead of clinging to a past that no longer exists?

> No one has ever become poor by giving.
>
> *Anne Frank,* The Diary of Anne Frank

Mike didn't ask me any more questions about the customer situation or why they canceled. His approach was a pattern interrupt that took me out of my head and into a new way of looking at things, because some stuff (like a customer decision or a catastrophic global event) can't be prevented. How we choose to respond is always within our grasp.

Thank you, Mike Heath, for your understanding. I pay it forward today, remembering to share what you gave freely to me, and I hope others can find the same.

I can still see that car. I can still see his face. But most of all, I can still feel the relief of what happens when a crisis is met with compassion.

> Be kind, for everyone you meet is fighting a harder battle.
>
> *Plato*

Simon Sinek, in a meeting with his team during the time of the corona-virus (https://bit.ly/listenup-sinek), said that the question in a time of crisis isn't "How are we going to get through this?" The real question is, "How are we going to *change* to get through this?"

Companies that succeed in the Age of the Customer use disruption as a time to reinvent themselves. To "change to get through this." To invent and innovate the future. And most importantly, to get out of a finite mindset.

Finite-minded leaders, according to Simon Sinek, in his video entitled "How do I lead with an Infinite Mindset" (https://bit.ly/listenup-sinek2), are threatened by uncertainty. They don't like surprises and they like to exert control over circumstances and situations, which is why we see a focus on short timeframes (quarters and years) in business.

If business is a game, do you view it with a finite or infinite mindset?

Finite games have known players, fixed rules, and agreed-upon objectives. Uncertainty, in a finite game, is a horrible thing. The unknown is a thing to avoid, because safety is found in the rules. However, Sinek notes, the mindset of "I followed the rules, I am safe," is meaningless when the very game has changed. Or when your customer changes the rules.

If there is disruption, rules and players and positions shift as well. While finite leaders find safety in regulations, Sinek says, infinite leaders find safety in *relationships*. Confronted with confusion, the leaders who will succeed are the ones who see the *connections* that matter. And then they leverage those relationships in new and powerful ways—ways that reshape the future.

How are you positioning yourself and your company to be the relationship that your customers crave in a time of crisis?

Why is it, Sinek wonders, that Amazon created the Kindle, and not the publishing industry? Because bookmakers were busy competing against other bookmakers, in a finite and fixed game, with known players, with known profitability and known probabilities of success. The e-reader changed the game and disrupted an entire industry.

One team—the e-reader team—was playing an infinite game. They weren't trapped by yesterday's constraints. "Remember, in the infinite game, you don't know all the players," Sinek says, prophetically.

You could be competing against other industries, other entrants, other possibilities. If you think about it, you could be leveraging those same possibilities for your company and for your partners. Want to play that game?

If business is an infinite game, uncertainties are doorways to opportunity. Remember, you don't know all the players! Finding the partners that can help you unlock those opportunities is how you win, especially when the rules have changed. During times of disruption, finding the right participants is the key to overcoming unseen challenges.

THE RIGHT PLAYERS AT THE RIGHT TIME

Herb Brooks was playing a finite game. Until he wasn't.

As a young man, Brooks had played hockey for the University of Minnesota, and the triumph of his life was being selected to join the U.S. Olympic Team at the ripe old age of 22.

Two weeks before going for gold, Brooks was cut from the team. He watched the U.S. hockey team—his team—from a barstool, instead of from the ice.

Years later, he became the hockey coach at Minnesota, his alma mater. Winning national championships thrust him onto the world stage when he was selected to coach the U.S. Olympic Team at the 1980 Winter Olympics.

A tryout was set up by the Olympic committee, providing Brooks the opportunity to see the best players in the country. "I don't want the best players," he says, "I want the right ones."

Brooks knew what others didn't: that there was something behind the statistics. Individual accomplishment wasn't the same as team development. In building his team, he made unorthodox decisions almost every step of the way.

Ralph Cox, the top college scorer in the country, from the University of New Hampshire, was cut from the team. That wasn't the only tough call the coach made. After being beaten in a tough game, Brooks didn't send his players to the locker room. He sent them back out on the ice and drilled them until some puked and the team doctor started to question his sanity. They kept skating until the lights were turned off in the arena. Brooks wouldn't quit, and he wanted his players to feel the same way.

Was there a method to his apparent madness? Was there direction inside of this disruption?

Herb Brooks wanted to beat the best hockey team in the world. He had a vision of just how he could do it. But would it work?

At the time, the Russian hockey team was unstoppable. They easily skated past the NHL All-Stars, and even beat the U.S. team 10–1 in a showcase match just days before the Lake Placid Olympics. Many of the Russian players had skated together for more than a decade. They were more cohesive. More skilled. Better trained.

The foe was unbeatable. The odds were insurmountable. And yet, Herb Brooks didn't believe the odds. He wanted to win.

His story, and the story of the heroes who brought victory to the United States, is the subject of the movie, *Miracle* (Disney, 2006). In Lake Placid, on a cold February day, the U.S. team managed to skate to a 4–3 lead. As the Soviets were out of options and the clock was winding down, sportscaster Al Michaels famously said, "Do you believe in miracles? YES!" From that call, the story of the U.S. Hockey Team became known as the "Miracle on the Ice."

So why are we discussing early 1980s hockey strategy in a book about customer listening? Because there's something I need you to hear. Something you need to know, now more than ever, and it doesn't involve skates and sticks. It's something that can help you to overcome the odds and make your own miracles.

How long does a miracle take? The Soviets had skated together for over a dozen years. The U.S. team had less than a year before they took on the best team in the world. Miracles can be quicker, smaller, and more common than we realize, because chaos can cloud our ability to see opportunity. Like innovation and creativity, there's no statute of limitations on miracles. The requirements are as simple as the recipe for that 1980 victory: Have a vision. Build the right team. Work like hell to bring your goals to life.

When you work hard toward your vision with the right players, you can achieve the impossible. Miracles aren't just something that happens on ice, or the subject of a Sunday school story. Some may associate miracles with some kind of religious experience, but as the Good Book says, "The Kingdom of Heaven is within you." Don't wait for the powers up above to bring you a miracle. You can go out and find one. Make one. Be one.

Divine intervention appears in random places or seems to: "It's a miracle that I beat the traffic today." "It's a miracle that the soufflé didn't flop." Remember what the preacher says? "The Lord helps those who help themselves."

Maybe you can't walk on water, but you can reach out a compassionate hand. You can listen. You can innovate. Even in the face of disruption, there's always something you can do. Even if that something is as simple as staying home and staying safe so that you can get back in the game when the time is right.

Everyday miracles. They're here right now. All around us.

Disruption causes denial. But miracles are there, hidden underneath a pile of fear, next to a load of wishing for what used to be.

Start with what is. Your customers and stakeholders will thank you for it, because, in the game of business, there's always disruption. Change. Competition.

There are winners and losers. What we learn from *Miracle* is what winning looks like:

Get the Right Players. Find the people who will work well together. Individual accomplishments aren't as important as the overall team performance.

Work Harder Than Anyone Else. Disruption requires greater focus, concentration, and commitment if you are going to make it through to the other side. Did you lose? Get back out on the ice. Go faster to go further. Never give up, no matter what the odds.

Find "Fresh Legs." Coach Brooks was famous for using weird metaphors that somehow made sense to his players. One of them was, "Legs feed the wolf," which (as best I can translate it) meant that the ability to get fresh legs on the ice was the key to speed, agility, and ultimately, victory. (Check out Kurt Russell's performance in the movie and let me know whether you get that same interpretation.) The disruptive game goes faster than you want it to. That was part of how the Soviets won—they played faster and more aggressive hockey than anybody else. Well, except for one team—and you know how that story ends. New entrants—new players with fresh perspectives—feed agility and offer fresh ideas (as well as fresh legs) for achieving your goals. By putting new guys on the ice, Brooks set the pace in his race toward victory. How are you finding fresh ideas?

Brooks shows us that playing an infinite game is the key to inviting in possibilities. From his early days of being cut from the team to leading the U.S. to unexpected victory, he dove into the unknown and used it as a competitive advantage. No one believed that a team of college kids could beat the Soviets—no one except Herb Brooks.

Disruption can be so powerful and calamitous that everything changes. Are you changing as well?

Are you adapting and getting fresh legs out on the ice? How are your customers doing? Bring compassion to your game; listen more, not less, in a time of crisis. Use the catalyst questions to make sure that you're seeing things in a new way and aligning yourself with your customers so that, together, you form a winning team.

The next chapter shows you exactly how to get the right people in the room so that you can build new pathways to victory. If you're willing to work to make your breaks, you can conquer any disruption by listening in still more powerful ways. Whether that disruption means overcoming a competitor with more experience or conquering a global crisis, the miracle that we all understand is that there is a way through this.

The question for the next chapter is: Are you willing to do what it takes?

CHAPTER 12

How to Win

"I've tried to get the decision reversed," I said to everyone on my team, via WebEx. "I've pulled every lever. I built a huge business case around how this can't happen. I've gone up two levels and talked to everyone. So here we are. No change. I am out of answers."

At Cisco, my team's entire function was to listen to customers and bring feedback to the company. My department had just been mentioned in CEO John Chamber's call with the shareholders as one of the fundamental pieces of the company's focus. We were foundational to the organization's growth. Untouchable. Bulletproof and future-proof. Until the day that I got the news.

I was given a 35 percent budget cut.

I couldn't believe the reality we were in. What was discussed for shareholders seemed in direct contradiction with the commitment to resources. My world was upside down, and I didn't know how to right the ship.

"That's why," I said to the screen, filled with stunned faces from all across the world, "I'm turning to you. We have to think about our business differently. I don't want to lay people off, but I will do what I have to do. The only way we can solve this is with your help."

Then I took the first step in seeing things in a new way. I listened.

A team member in Denver said that she noticed that the company was thinking and working and operating in silos. Cisco had grown, in large part, by acquisition, often leaving acquired companies to "do what they did best" and trying to minimize the kind of oversight that would monkey with the business. So a team from one division, or even one product, would do surveys and deliver the results on the survey in isolation.

Another member from North Carolina expanded on the idea. There was a separate team that conducted data analysis based on the surveys. Another team did focus groups, my lead engineer in Palo Alto shared, and we hire a lot of third parties to get this work done.

121

What I was hearing was a story about silos, separation, and complexity. What could we do, I wondered, to make this easier for everyone involved?

Instead of thinking, "You play offense, I'll play defense, and somebody else can be the goalie," we came together as a team. We created service at scale.

We started to think horizontally instead of vertically. We went to key stakeholders and said, "We can help you to do a survey of the people who are buying Product X, and then we will talk with individuals who make comments in the open-ended questions. If you like, we will follow up with a couple of focus groups."

The pitch was a simple one: As an internal asset within the company, we could provide more holistic insight than an outside firm. We had the ability and insight to see across divisions, product lines, and geographies. Plus, we were a one-stop shop. We had a done-for-you solution that was better, faster, and almost always less expensive than hiring an outside firm.

Various divisions and executives within the company began hiring us almost immediately. We went from a cost center with a 35 percent budget cut to (wait for it) . . . a profit center.

But we didn't stop there, because some folks still said that they didn't need outside help for a small customer study. So the team developed off-the-shelf survey tools—a list of questions with online tools to make administration easy. We realized that if we were going to have different factions doing surveys on their own, there should be a standardized platform for coordination, branding, and visibility company wide.

So one of my team members built it. She reasoned that using this standardized tool would be something for which we could charge customers, and a fee of $19.95 a month was suggested. That seems reasonable, right? Less than 20 bucks to get access to standardized, branded survey tools? Well, the company agreed, and multiple entities from around the globe signed up for our simple service.

Did I mention that the company had 71,000 employees at the time? Guess what: If you can get 10,000 of them to give you $19.95 a month, that's a revenue stream of nearly $2.4 million a year.

We were back in business.

We hired contractors, upgraded our tools, and reshaped our business to fulfill our CEO's promise. We went from thinking that we had to cut people to fit the budget to a new mindset: We re-created the budget.

When funding was cut, we figured out a way to be self-funding.

How did we do it? It started when we stopped wringing our hands and put our hands on the wheel. That's what it feels like when you decide to drive your own destiny.

It's easy to fall into the trap of "being number one." You are featured on an analyst call and you make up a mythology around who you are and just how important you are. Have you been there? While we were enjoying the story that we were telling ourselves, the world changed. More than a third of our budget went up in smoke, and we had our foot on the brake. We didn't know what we were going to do.

Being at your peak can be a dangerous position, especially if you are patting yourself on the back when the other shoe drops. The best way that leaders can stay in front of a challenge, no matter what it is, is through connection with other like-minded leaders.

Right now, every CEO wants to call another CEO and say, "Dude (or Dudette), what are you doing? Do you have the magic formula? Are you freaking out? Because I am freaking out. Should I be? What's working for you? How are you talking to employees?"

THE CUSTOMER ADVISORY BOARD

Every leader who cares about winning wants to meet another company that has survived this kind of disruption or implemented that kind of product. The Catalyst Question asks, *"How can I help you right now . . . to get those answers?"*

The answer is a *Customer Advisory Board*, a coalition of leaders from noncompeting companies coming together to discuss important and hyper-relevant business issues. These Councils and Boards go beyond online case studies or exchanging executive phone numbers. Because there's one thing that every executive, everywhere, wants—a backstage pass.

I'm not talking about getting a selfie with Bono or Benioff. While it's always good to know a real rock star, the backstage pass gives you insight into what's coming next. You see the other members of the band, and you get a handle on what the inside looks like. You see how they make the music from an inside perspective. The Customer Advisory Board is your top customer's backstage pass.

There's enormous value in being able to talk with other leaders at companies with whom you don't compete so that you can listen to new perspectives and ideas. And that's exactly why I've spent the last few years focused on Customer Feedback Councils (aka customer advisory boards, in other words, your backstage pass).

Typically conducted as an invitation-only event, delivered as a dinner or similar function (although Zoom can work in a pinch, if you're wondering), you set up a high-impact agenda for a high-caliber audience. In a moment, I'll explain how to set up the agenda and conduct the meeting so that everyone comes away with exceptional value. But first, there are three things that you MUST do when you assemble a group of companies, customers, and clients in an executive-level advisory session:

1. Put away the PowerPoint!
2. Put away the PowerPoint!!
3. Put away the PowerPoint!!!

The purpose of the Advisory Board is simple: building relationships. You are there to listen and to create the type of one-of-a-kind crosstalk that these leaders can't find anywhere else.

Remember, you've called the customers together to ask for their advice: they are the advisors, not you. Don't deliver a bait-and-switch sales pitch, or you'll be dead before you even begin. It's counterintuitive, but not counterproductive: The customers actually set the agenda for the Council, not you.

PRESS PAUSE ON POWERPOINT

Focus on fostering partnerships, not bedazzling people with your snazzy slides. Relationship-building (and the resultant listening opportunities that arise from your event) can't be found anywhere else. That insight is rarer than a ruby and even more priceless.

Resist the urge to roll out your new products, unless you are going to listen up long enough to cultivate feedback around them. The Customer Advisory Council is about listening, not promoting. Don't shove slides down your panel's throat to see how long it takes until they all revolt. The very idea is already revolting. You are off your agenda, and you will miss the real value in the conversation.

Your customers want to know each other—they want the access they can't get anywhere else; they want to go backstage. Through effective listening, you can foster the dialogue and deliver agile answers, which is the real value of the Customer Councils and Advisory Boards.

The less you talk, the better off you'll be.

After a Salesforce advisory dinner that I conducted in London, a senior executive at a major telecom provider came up to me. "I've never been in a meeting like this before," he said, his speech pattern reminding me of the one and only Michael Caine. "Why . . . why didn't you pitch us on any of your products? I mean, we sat here for two hours and you didn't talk about yourself at all! It was amazing!" He went on to say that it was one of the best and most valuable evenings he had spent in his nearly three decades in the industry. What he had learned in those 120 minutes were things he never could have gathered from a slide deck. His gratitude matches up with feedback that I've received all over the world. Because the value in the Council is in two places: (1) access and (2) relationships—it's never on the projector screen.

The other big mistake that I see, and it happens all too often, is the do-nothing syndrome. Maybe you are familiar with the symptoms? It looks like this:

■ Fabulously valuable conversations take place as part of an Advisory Board session.

- Somebody takes notes.
- Notes are then submitted to customers who attended the session and to the executives who presented or facilitated the event.
- Executive assistants are involved and maybe even a Chief of Staff.
- The resulting information provides insight into what executives at the companies that make up the top 20 percent of your revenues would like to know more about.
- Fewer than 1 percent of the people in your organization will ever see or hear that information.
- The value of such conversations is almost impossible to express because it is ENORMOUS.
- And then: Nothing happens.

Emails are not action. Sharing may be caring, but if you really care you'd take the time to compassionately create real service around the event. Don't stop with caring; make a decision to be compelling. *Compelling means that you inspire action.* And you take action. Here's how to turn Listening Councils and Advisory Boards to your competitive advantage, step by step.

C-Sparks: Start the Conversation

How to Conduct a Customer Advisory Council That's Compelling, Clear, and Cohesive

Personalize the Agenda

Ask your customers what they would like to know from your company in the sessions. Gather that feedback and follow up wherever it's necessary, because this kind of listening is pure gold. At the same time, ask your executive leaders who will be in the room, or who have a stake in the conversation: What would you like to know from our customers? Gather this feedback and keep it close, because you'll be using it soon.

The Approach Is to Coach

Meet with each of the executives from your company who will be attending the event. Ask them to reach out to the customers who will be in attendance. That's right, there's going to be a conversation before the big conversation, and this one will pay big dividends if you do it right. You coach your

(continued)

(continued)

executive team that their conversation is required, and it is also simple. The conversation shares that the company is listening. Your executive restates the feedback from the customer and asks one additional question: Can you give me a couple of questions that you'd love to ask our CEO (or COO or CMO or CHRO or whoever will be in the room) when he or she is present-ing? You capture those questions and correlate: What ideas are showing up? What do these questions have in common?

Gather and Distribute

As you have identified common themes by now from these exec questions, summarize your findings with your company's leaders who will be attend-ing the event. "Here are the five or six issues that are top of mind." Remem-ber, they are top of mind for your customers. That's the agenda you want to foster here—keep everyone focused on how and where the customers will find value in the meeting. It's counterintuitive, but that's the source of the ultimate value for your company as well. Notice that, if you are following me so far, you are listening before you start listening. You are expressing the agenda, shaping the agenda, and creating relevance and direction for the entire executive team.

Sing from the Same Sheet Music

When you publish the agenda in advance, you list top-of-mind questions from customers for this session, and then you let the customers know what the execs want to know from them. That approach gives them a chance to go to other people in their organization and say, "Hey Shanna, the CEO of DreamWorks is going to come present, and he's going to talk about the future of digital and if you can, yeah, ask him one question, I mean, what would you want to know?"

Resist Primal Urges

In the meeting, you need a rock star facilitator. I'm talking about somebody who has the brains, chutzpah, and gravitas to welcome the participants in the right context (namely, restating the questions that have been gathered, debated, and established prior to the meeting). And then, the true rock star resists the primal urge to data dump upon all the participants. The rock star facilitator leaves the PowerPoint roped and tied up in the barn, never to be released. The rock star facilitator is the one who, when a well-intentioned exec starts into a sales pitch, says, "I want to make sure that the customers leave with the answers that matter most. So let's press pause for a minute. Let's go to the first question and follow our agenda." Because the rock star knows what mere mortals often forget: PowerPoint is not listening. Pitching is not productive (in this context). When you resist the urge to speechify or sell, you discover something new and even more valuable. You might just find direction. Guidance. Insight. Dare I say it? Genius.

The Customer Advisory Council is an opportunity to bring people together in a powerful way. And I'm not just talking about your largest customers. I'm talking about how you, as a company, show up in the conversation. Are you clear on the agenda? The objectives? Are both of those things aligned around your customers? Do you have a facilitator who's enough of a rock star to keep everything focused on the right questions?

By now, you know what questions to ask. You've seen how to facilitate the Big Impact Question, the Genius Question, the Catalyst Questions, and more. It's time to bring people together and tailor your insights to their needs. Listen to what customers really want to know. Have enough confidence in your company and your executive presence to let the folks who matter most drive the agenda. And commit to focusing your Council on the voice that drives the business: the voice of the customer.

Brian Solis is the Global Innovation Evangelist at Salesforce and an internationally recognized keynote speaker, author, and thought leader. He says simply that companies that want to win aren't focused on customer experience. They are focused on *the customer's experience.*

That small apostrophe "s" points toward ownership. Today, organizations are tapping into advanced online tools and data mining to discover new ways of impacting the customer journey. And for companies that want to win, it's time to take ownership of new insights. Those insights lie ahead, as I want to share what Brian has shared with me. Because innovation, I've discovered, is how we get back to the future.

CHAPTER 13

Moving at the Speed of the Customer

Is your company biased?

The fact of the matter is, yes. Yes, it is.

And, just in case you are wondering: you are, too.

Bias is a fact of life. A simpler word for "bias" is preference, and we all have preferences. Writing with your left or right hand, for example, is a simple example of preference. So is eating broccoli. Or not. These biases are simple choices, where no person (or broccoli) is damaged, ignored, or underserved.

But what about your customers' preferences? Knowing those biases could be valuable information. Yet, we often think of bias as harmful. Hurtful. Something to avoid.

So is bias a good thing or a bad thing?

Moving at the speed of the customer means seeing beyond bias, capitalizing on preferences, and making sure that no one is left behind. When some preferences are ignored (that would be a "hidden bias") your customers suffer—sometimes, even with tragic consequences.

That's the message from Yana Kakar (https://bit.ly/listenup-kakar), Global Managing Partner Emeritus at Dalberg, as she explains how key metrics were missed in the development of the seatbelt. "Did you know," she asks, from her home office in New York City, "that when a woman is in a serious car crash, she is nearly 50 percent more likely to be injured than a man? And nearly 20 percent more likely to die?"

Kakar is half Australian, half Indian, and a dual citizen of Canada and the United States. She holds an MBA from Wharton. She's an executive whose diverse experience defies categories. Since 2013, she's served as the head of the firm at Dalberg, a company whose mission is to solve the world's most pressing problems while developing global leaders. Her voice is both confident and comforting. In another life, I imagine that she might have been a voiceover artist, but only for ads that projected nothing but calm and trust.

A member of the Brookings Institute's Global Leadership Council and active in the Young Presidents Organization (YPO), she advises across the public, private, and nonprofit sectors, and she is especially well known for helping leaders in business and in finance to drive performance through, not in spite of, the integration of social impact and environmental sustainability into their business models and investment portfolios. Her conversation is easily peppered with references to civil society, NGOs, and the challenges facing Africa—a reflection of her global perspective as well as her concern. Together with her firm, she works to maximize positive social and environmental outcomes, with a focus on gender, youth, and socially responsible investment (SRI). From disease tracking in West Africa to prototyping labs for microfinance, the company's emphasis is on conscious capitalism, doing business in a way that's doing good.

"But higher mortality rates for women in car crashes are not doing anybody any good," she says. "Crash test dummies were designed based on an average-sized man," Kakar continues. "Not taking into account that women weigh less and tend to be shorter, thus moving the seat further forward. This oversight meant greater risk of injury." When women are in car crashes, they tend to be in one of the passenger seats. "Because men drive more, particularly if you think about different countries culturally," she says, perhaps referring to Saudi Arabia, where women were not granted the right to drive until 2018. Despite the country opening seven driving schools, according to a *New York Times* article from 2019 (https://bit.ly/listenup-saudiarabia), the country does not publish or offer any statistics on the number of women drivers in the country. But no matter where you are in the world, automobile manufacturers who don't design for female drivers might be the real dummies in this story.

"Nobody applied a gender lens to the solution [of seat belts]," Yana continues. In her conferences and sponsored events, attendees better buckle up: There is a deliberate effort to create what she calls a "cross-section" conversation. "It's vital that we apply a gender lens when we're doing anything for the clients we serve. We've changed our entire analytical approach to our work, via a public commitment. Because, for us, there's no such thing as gender-blind."

THE VALUE IN BIAS

Perspective and preference matter. Just as you would test for the experience on a mobile device versus a desktop, adapting the journey to the customer's perspective is the only approach that matters. While bias can create blind spots, understanding who your customers are and how they are using your products is vital to creating a personalized and productive journey.

Bias that excludes is a fool's errand, ending only in missed opportunities, disappointment, and (in the case of the seat belt example) tragedy. "We understand that people want to be heard," Yana explains. "Just because I think the data is self-evident is a limiting bias. The learning at Dalberg, for each of our 27 offices, is to listen to the partner's concerns and not place a value judgment on them. That's quite difficult, you know," she says, lowering her voice to describe the situation she doesn't want to indulge. "Listening to somebody and then not filing things away. Really listening, not just rapidly categorizing."

That kind of categorization is hard to avoid. At least that's what the Dunning-Kruger effect shows us. The *Dunning-Kruger effect* describes how people overestimate their competence or cognitive abilities and don't realize the error of their ways. The issue isn't just that people make poor choices from erroneous conclusions, it's also that they are unable to recognize those errors.[1]

Lack of Knowledge

In the Dunning-Kruger effect, the less someone knows about a topic, the more likely he or she is to have strong opinions about that topic. This means that if you are arguing a point with someone who has beliefs that are not rooted in facts, that person will stick to an opinion, even when presented with evidence to the contrary. That person will also disregard expert opinions. The person may tell you that the expert opinion is "fake," the expert was "paid off" to give that opinion, or he or she may just talk over you so that you can't get your facts heard. Since you can't prove that something didn't happen, you walk away frustrated, while the other person is more entrenched in his or her beliefs.

Misinformation Endorsement

The Dunning-Kruger effect means that people will endorse erroneous information if it fits their opinions. Misinformation endorsement means that someone doesn't do the work in researching sources to see whether they are legitimate. It also means that independent research is not done, so beliefs are not challenged by other information.

---

[1] Components of the Dunning-Kruger effect from *Psychology Today*

A misinterpretation of the facts can occur when you experience *selection bias* (also called "survivor bias"). Here's how selection bias is described in *Forbes* (https://bit.ly/listenup-survivor):

> *"Selection bias is a misinterpretation of the odds, resulting in poor management strategies. For example, the probability of becoming famous, according to mathematician Samuel Arbesman, is about 0.000086 percent. However, how you define being famous (YouTube? Movies? Silicon Valley?) might shift that statistic. Nevertheless, the odds are slim—approximately 1 in 10,000 people are famous, regardless of the arena you choose. But wait a minute. If you are Brad Pitt, PewDiePie, or Elon Musk, there's a different equation at play. For each of them, the probability of being famous is 100 percent. The odds are exactly 1."*

The article continues to ask this intriguing question:

> "If two different people take the exact same actions under different circumstances, will they get the same results? If you said Yes, you're suffering from selection bias."

The journey, for you, your customer, and your leadership team is always a personal one. Overlooking the personal nature of the journey creates a simple misunderstanding that arises from hidden bias.

Personal bias, on many levels, can be dangerous when it is undiscovered. Insidious. Limiting. Preference isn't poisonous, but lack of awareness can be deadly.

If you know you're left-handed and that you like broccoli, that's really neither a good thing nor a bad thing. What's really good is that these facts are known to you. So, too, if you know that certain customers prefer accessing your website via a mobile device, this can inform your behavior and your decisions. What you don't see in yourself—and in your customers—is a reason to pause. To consider. To explore greater inquiry, not snap to judgment.

When is personal preference (bias) unwise? When it causes blind spots.

One of the classic impediments to the leadership conversation, Kakar points out, are two little words: "What about # . . . ?" It's a conversation-killing condition often described as "what-about-ism." This bias can shut down conversations, derail agendas, and disengage both alignment and inquiry. "The minute you offer an insight into business in China, someone says, 'Ok, but what about Japan?' or when I say, 'Gender is important,' and someone says, 'But what about minorities? What about the disabled? What about special needs?'"

From a place of rapid conclusion (a fancy way of saying, "snap judgment" with an extra helping of bias thrown in), we miss the opportunity to explore. To discover. To engage with what we discussed in earlier chapters: the beginner's mindset.

When is bias wise, informative, and expansive? When you fully understand it.

Here's how to help your team and your customers to access a greater level of understanding—with some powerful questions (that aren't really questions at all) thrown in for good measure.

C-Sparks: Two Small Words, One Big Impact

In the world of improvisational theater, every performer understands two words. Improv is a place where a simple scenario is given to two performers, and suddenly they have to create a scene from a simple description. Made famous at places like Chicago's Second City and on television shows like *Whose Line Is It Anyway?*, improvisation asks performers to accept and believe in a circumstance—no matter how unexpected or outrageous. What are the two words that every improv performer uses in order to create something innovative? The answer is, "Yes, and. . ."

Amy Poehler, my absolute favorite actress on the always-brilliant *Parks and Recreation,* is a master of improvisation. In a video interview with the CBC (https://youtu.be/KyjpncepVuM), she explains how improv performers use "yes, and" as a form of agreement when improvising, because you have to support your partner, whether you are on *Saturday Night Live* or trying to maximize your customer's experience. In improv, you have to accept the construct or the scenario first if you are going to expand on anything. From a place of agreement comes expansion. Denial, or "whatabout-ism," is a deflection and a rejection of the premise. Without agreement, the scene stops cold before it has even begun.

That's true in business, too. While it's important to be able to share various viewpoints (and not every conversation ends in agreement), possibilities often begin with a "Yes." That first yes is the acknowledgment of the situation, without judgment, and a willingness to explore a particular scenario, issue, or circumstance. Note that acknowledgment isn't the same as agreement. I can see the situation and still hope for a different outcome. But what path is most effective for reaching the kind of outcome that serves everyone involved?

(continued)

(continued)

- Find opportunities when you can explore "yes, and" for yourself. What would change if you adapted or adopted this approach?
- When you consider the world of business—your world and your customers—is that scene unfolding like a scripted drama, or is it filled with elements of improvisation? Assuming that life is scripted or that it follows a predetermined pattern is perhaps the biggest misconception ever. In my experience, and in yours too I suspect, even the most well-thought-out customer journey has some unexpected turns—some eddies, as we explored in a previous chapter. In her autobiography, *Yes Please* (Dey Street, 2014)—yep, it's a take on the idea of "yes, and"—Amy Poehler writes, "If you can surf your life rather than plant your feet, you will be happier."
- What is your analysis of preference? What can you do today to identify the hidden preferences that create dangerous personal bias, and by extension, offer that same insight to your customers? The effectiveness of the seat belt might depend on your answer. We've explored multiple levels of inquiry, from Big Impact Questions to the Genius Question, and multiple points in between. Where do you need to apply a deeper level of curiosity, applying these ideas to lift the veil of unseen bias around your business?

Ray Wang (pronounced "WAHNG") explains that a deeper understanding of preference can lead to accelerated growth and new opportunity. He is Principal Analyst and CEO at Constellation Research, based in Silicon Valley. He's worked at Altimeter, Forrester, Oracle, EY, and Deloitte, and today he advises Global 2000 companies on business strategy and technology.

In his book, *Disrupting Digital Business: Create an Authentic Experience in the Peer-to-Peer Economy* (Harvard Business Review Press, 2015), he notes that the recession of 2008 didn't slow the pace of change. That worldwide disruption actually had the opposite effect. "The recession was a catalyst and an accelerant. . . . The key to companies' success will be to develop disruptive digital business models of their own."

As I write these words, the impact of the current global economic contraction is a complete unknown. But dealing with the unknown—improvising new solutions—is something that companies have been doing since business was invented. The emphasis is on transformation. Wang explains it like this:

"Customers know that we're no longer selling products or services— we're keeping brand promises. . . . This is more than just a drive for incremental improvement or even a special ops team of ninjas or tiger teams. Organizations must build a culture with a transformational mindset. Transformation-minded organizations do more than just challenge the status quo: they try to understand the root cause of the problem. They want to understand the possibilities. They want to push the limits.

"What we long for is right-time relevancy. Delivery of the right information, at the right time, in the right mode, for the right situation, with the right priority level is what we're after. And how we get there is through context. Context is the key driver of right-time relevancy.

"We're at a point where we no longer merely sell products or deliver on services. In the digital world, customers require businesses to focus on delivering authentic experiences and outcomes."

WHY YOU HAVE TO EARN THE CUSTOMER

What is it that you need to try in order to adapt to the changes in your marketplace? When the rules have changed, or maybe even the whole game, you've got to get closer than ever to the people who matter most: your customers.

"If you earned a customer relationship," Wang shares, "and I say 'earned' much more so than 'owned,' because you don't ever 'own' a customer. But you can *earn* one. You can earn a relationship with a customer's food business without ever owning a kitchen," he points out, with a nod to GrubHub. "Or own their transportation business without buying a single car or truck." It's the Uber-ization of the market. "The reality is, you basically are proving your value every day. Customers are trading loyalty for value. Customers are trading loyalty for a status. Customers are trading loyalty for price. Customers are trading loyalty for convenience, and that clearly tells you that you have to *earn* a customer."

What are you doing to earn your customer? Because ownership—the illusion of ownership—can cause you to rest on your laurels. During times of rapid change and upheaval, what you take for granted just might get taken away.

OWNING THE JOURNEY

Brian Solis says that the key to keeping your customers is to use data in an empathetic way.

Solis is a digital anthropologist who specializes in understanding how disruptive technology is driving the future. He's the author of eight books, including *Lifescale: How to Live a More Creative, Productive, and Happy Life* (Wiley, 2019), *WTF?: What's the Future of Business?: Changing the Way Businesses Create Experiences* (Wiley, 2013), and *X: The Experience When Business Meets Design* (Wiley, 2015).

"Data-driven empathy is the idea that we can use data in its purest, most enlightening way to see the *humanity*—the human on the other side of the ones and zeros," he explains via conference call from his office in Northern California. "That way, we can make decisions beyond 'the next best action on the best device' at the right time. But also, taking things a step further: What should that next best action be?"

For the last decade, Solis has been talking about Generation C—the connected customer that defies an age-based demographic in favor of a psychographic one. Because you can't blame connectivity on youth. "Gen C isn't an age group," he shares (https://bit.ly/listenup-genc), "it's a way of life." Embracing the digital world is the psychological hallmark of Gen C, and connectivity (often via multiple devices at once) is one of many interconnected characteristics.

"Have companies defined what's going to be relevant to Gen C?" he inquires. That's where the "Customer's Experience" (with an apostrophe "s") comes into play.

"Most organizations get caught in the psychology of bias," he affirms. "In a world of AI and machine learning, now we're teaching algorithms and systems how to carry out those biases at scale. The whole nature of biases is that we don't see them."

Are you talking about improving personalization? "Humanization," he says. "Allowing ourselves to go back further to realize that actually the technology is helping us to build these incredible bridges. Digital can help us to better understand how people are communicating, how people are making decisions, and what people value."

NEW VALUE, NEW SOLUTIONS

Solis continues, "If you don't take the apostrophe 's' approach, you bring natural human bias, or cognitive bias, into the conversation. The dialogue is tainted by the frustrations that we have, the politics, and the egos that we have to deal with every single day."

By definition, biased conversation is not customer centric. "We had the best intent," he says, shaking his head as he reflects on numerous client interactions, "but we're actually bringing ourselves—our bias—into those conversations. That bias leads to iteration, which is just making investments that build upon the existing experiences. Nothing wrong with that, it's just that you get iterative design. Iterative is not innovative. Innovation is when you create new value."

Every customer at every organization has that "moment of truth," where he or she has to engage to find information, whether it's shipment delivery data, interoperability, instructions, or whatever. By visiting a web page, engaging a chat bot, or dialing into a frustrating IVR system, the "customer's experience" is a reflection of the company's bias toward information, interaction, and the use of technology.

Some companies, Solis says, actually use technology to get further away from people. Then these organizations create a series of metrics to track their performance using these technological tools, in other words, recognizing and rewarding themselves for getting further away from the people who matter most.

Congratulations on being efficient and using technological tools. Just one quick follow-up question: How's your customer doing?

"None of those metrics looked at humanity. How did someone feel when we engaged her? How quickly could we help him feel better or address his needs?" Solis wonders aloud, echoing the voice of the customer. Technology, at the speed of the customer, isn't just a tool for reducing cost or increasing margins. The promise of technology lies within an investment designed to redefine customer engagement—to personalize the experience so that it drives loyalty, growth, and social sharing in a way that goes beyond intention, to action. The bias that's particularly insidious and dangerous? He calls it the "experience divide." The divide has two parts:

1. There's what we (the company) think is the way the world works.
2. There's the way the customer wants the world to work.

Somewhere in the middle is the Venn diagram of how customers and your company come together. That Venn diagram appears when you erase bias. "The first thing that's needed," Solis explains, "is to get really, really curious." He stops to demonstrate what he's about to say next. "What we're talking about is taking a pause and taking time to ask some better questions."

Because AI gets into trouble when asking the same questions, you're developing datasets around the wrong space. Just as an incredibly detailed map of Cleveland won't help you when what you really need is located in South Boston, or even Shaker Heights.

Creating a culture of disruption is the way to deal with disruptive times, to accelerate to the speed of the customer. And that acceleration comes by design—designing the culture of the organization around curios-ity. Improvisation. And a commitment to reveal bias and preference wher-ever possible, so that understanding guides both technology and humanity to new results.

C-Sparks: Creating a Culture of Customer Centricity

Customer centricity is about truly understanding someone you don't know. I can only imagine what you're thinking, "Wait a minute! I know my customer!"

Pause for just a moment. Is your bias showing?

1. SEEK AND FIND

Intentionally seek what it is that you don't know. How would you approach your customers if you didn't know them? What would you say, share, and do? What if you didn't have an elaborate avatar chart on your wall? What if you approached the conversation—the journey—as if for the first time?

2. NOTICE WHAT YOU NOTICE

Where are you seeing iteration within your Customer Experience func-tion? Where do you see innovation? What patterns or circumstances do you notice that provide for greater innovation, and how can you build your organization and your culture around transformational results?

3. A BIG JOURNEY IN ONE SMALL STEP

Innovation and transformation seem like grand gestures: great in concept, but mysterious in execution. The crazy thing is that innovation is never more than one thought away. That's true for transformation as well. By definition, innovation doesn't come from what you already know. Shed-ding bias is how innovation is revealed. There's no experience required in order to innovate—you don't need a master's degree or a corner office. New ideas are available any time you want to access them. Press pause. Invite innovation. Look for it. Reward it. Get enough people sharing a new way of looking at things. That's exactly how you'll transform your culture, and your customer experience as well.

HUMAN-CENTERED DESIGN

There's no doubt that the amount of noise is increasing exponentially, driving more and more distraction. Gen C has too many tabs open in their browser, Slack requires your immediate attention, and don't even get me started on texts and Twitter. How do you connect in a distracted world and engage with your customer?

"Break down the journey into bite-sized pieces," Solis says. "Make your way to identifying *micro moments*."

Micro moments focus on intention, not demographics, because, as Solis shared in a post on *Forbes* (https://bit.ly/listenup-solis), demographics can be deceptive. And not always predictive.

Consider, for example, two men, both born in England in 1948. They are both wealthy, married for the second time, and each has two children. They enjoy spending winter holidays in the Alps. Both of these men love dogs.

One man is Prince Charles, the heir to the British throne. The other is Ozzy Osbourne.

Demographics can be a bit of a crazy train. That's why micro moments matter more: because they point to future intent, not past history, inside the context that matters most—the customer journey.

Think sentences instead of paragraphs. A 16-second video instead of a 5-minute one. "You're essentially delivering messages for people in the way that they need to see them," Solis explains, "and inviting them to that next step."

Personal communications apps like Instagram, Snapchat, and TikTok rely on a persuasive and micro moment design. While I'm not suggesting that we use TikTok to market ERP systems or explain industrial logistics, there's an opportunity to get granular using AI tools. Because AI can actually help you to *quiet* the noise.

> "By taking UX (user experience) and UI (user interface) persuasive design techniques, we create what I call HX, which is a human-experience design."

Solis is describing his vision for the future: a human-centric experience designed to exist outside of bias but inside of a technologically advanced data engine. "I'm talking about blending the better parts of those design intentions and bringing people into the moment," rather than losing the moment to the multitude of distractions that vie for everyone's attention.

"We have to now expect that state of mind (how we talk, how we communicate, how we design touch points) is designed for micro moments. The available capacity is for customers to only be engaged for a split second, and then move them along."

Because in the same way that you can distract a customer, you can pull them out of distraction. The idea is that you're leading them back toward something that is in their best interest.

In an interview with David Baekholm (https://bit.ly/listenup-solis1), Senior Vice President of HomeAway, Solis discovered some eye-opening statistics. The company got granular on their customer's journey, discovering multiple micro moments where they could create new engagement and drive new levels of influence. The end result? A 200 percent lead conversion increase in just 12 days.

Rapid results. Powerful acceleration. That's business at the speed of the customer, and the driver is human-centric design. Looking specifically at the challenges and the eddies within the customer journey, where do you see problems? How can you redirect your tech tools, like machine learning and AI, to identify those micro moments and develop new ways of engagement?

That innovation is within your grasp, right now.

"The challenge isn't the technology," Solis says, prophetically. "It's the humanity."

In the next chapter, we'll look at how companies are synthesizing the customer experience into a new kind of brand value, designed to add value to a company's top line. New discoveries are attracting the attention of the M&A community. What's the impact of listening, when investors, stakeholders, and other evaluators see the customer as your largest asset?

CHAPTER 14

Look Who's Talking

"**M**arriage Counselors exist for a reason," Bruce Kidd says. The former Director for Entrepreneurship and Small Business for the Indiana Economic Development corporation sits in a red leather chair in his home office. Behind him, white shelves are filled with hundreds of CDs, two yearbooks from Purdue, and pictures of his kids. A wooden box is open on the first shelf, but the cigars inside are hidden from view. In the corner, a 140-pound Italian Mastiff named Bella is sleeping on a sheepskin pillow. The sunlight from the window streams across his salt-and-pepper goatee. I wonder, have I stumbled into an uncomfortable marriage confession?

I hear a knock on his office door. His wife, Chris, walks in and waves at me. She sets down a fresh cup of coffee. "Don't get used to this kind of service," she says to Bruce, smiling as she gives a half-hearted push to that red leather chair. Bruce is a big guy, so the chair moves a millimeter or two maybe. But the little push gives him a big smile. "I won't," Bruce says to his quarantine companion, as he thanks her for the kindness.

Kidd is a Senior Account Executive at KSM Consulting. A specialist in mergers and acquisitions, he started his career developing entrepreneurial businesses at EY, formerly known as Ernst & Young. A former executive in residence for Purdue Ventures, an incubator at the Big 10 university in northwest Indiana, he's been helping business owners create and transfer value his entire career.

Chris slips out, closing the office door behind her. Bruce tries the coffee.

"I have a good friend who's a marriage counselor," he says as he puts down the mug. "My friends have gone to her because, in the relationship, things just happened where somebody can't say what he or she really wants to say to a spouse because it will cause too much havoc." Yet, those things need to be said—we all understand that. Having an objective listener can make a huge difference.

"The marriage counselor creates a platform—an environment—where someone can share without belittling their spouse. Because, the idea goes, 'I'm really talking to the marriage counselor, not to my spouse,' "

Important and potentially difficult messages are best shared in a safe and controlled environment, where people are much more likely to be open and honest. That honesty is the centerpiece of counseling.

The power of a neutral third party is an important concept in the business world as well, because having the right questions and identifying the right customer isn't the whole story. You have to consider who's asking the questions, if you want to get to the candid, frank, and actionable answers. The right questions—the right information—have to be addressed by the right person. You have to look at who's talking.

Because people will tell a marriage counselor things that they won't or can't tell each other. Bruce would know. He's kind of a marriage counselor for CEOs. "Good questions alone aren't enough," he explains, as he dives into a hypothetical scenario that he's seen many times.

"What happens all too often is that Bill calls Joe, his customer in Dayton. Bill says, 'How are we doing, Joe?' Joe, the customer, says, 'Oh, you're doing fine, Bill. Yeah, you guys. Yep. You're good.' "

It's a version of the truth, but it's not the whole truth. Because Joe and Bill know each other, their relationship is what psychologists would call "overdetermined." That's a fancy way of saying complicated: Their history makes it hard to talk truth, especially if that truth is hard to hear. See, Joe knows that Bill's daughter just got accepted into NYU. Bill knows that Joe loves any kind of barbeque, and he's got a six handicap on the golf course. They're pals. They've got a business relationship, strengthened by a personal one, and that relationship matters to both of them. That overdetermined relationship is the source of their mutual success. And it's also why neither one can be fully honest with the other.

Bill asks his friend, Joe, to rate the company's performance—and his performance—on a one to five scale. Do you think Bill is going to get a three from his friend, even if he deserves it?

Bruce explains, "Joe's gonna give his friend some good vibes. 'Excellent' is what the scores will say, because good scores are in the best interest of the relationship," Bruce continues, as he leans back in his chair, "except when they are not."

When the wrong person asks the right questions, the response gets sanitized. Filtered. Softened. Sales reps are interested in "all fives." Sales leaders are interested in "all truth," even if it's hard to hear.

When you take the sales rep or the frontline person out of the equation, it's a completely different discussion.

FINDING VALUE

Picture this scenario: Tim is a 67-year-old CEO living in Michigan. He's worked hard to build his business, and it's time to move on. He wants to sell and move to the Florida panhandle. What's the first step? Before he calls a realtor in Destin, Florida, he's got to get his corporate house in order. Soon he'll begin searching for potential buyers—a quest that has to be conducted discreetly, so as not to alarm his employees or his customers.

He'll ask his accountants and CFO to prepare all the necessary documents, pull some details from his bank, run some detailed inventory reports, and more. Imagine that things progress, and a buyer shows some interest. The buyer asks for the financials and likes what she sees. But she also has some questions about the quality of the asset, the value of the company, the relationships that are the key to that value.

I'm not talking about investigating the profiles of the executive leadership team—that's boilerplate M&A stuff. I'm talking about the customer set that's the lifeblood of the business.

In a scenario like this, when buyers want to know just how much a company is worth, Bruce Kidd shows up. Because you need to have a marriage counselor if you want a relationship to work.

Sending in somebody from "Mergers and Acquisitions Incorporated" is a great way to alert employees that something is up. And poking around in a company's customer set can produce panic. The customer wonders: Is our supplier about to be sold? What's going to happen to our relationship if somebody buys this really important vendor? Should I look for other resources? Should I pass on the three-year contract they just put in front of me? Uncertainty kills deals, and dealmakers work hard to maintain confidentiality.

"We come in and we sit down with the company's customers," Bruce explains. "Our approach is to speak on behalf of the company in Michigan the CEO wants to sell." The impulse for the conversation isn't something alarming. The conversation is conducted in an effort to create a better relationship.

"We come in and let the customers know that we need to ask a series of questions. Because every company can be better, and your supplier in Michigan wants to know how, we want your candid feedback." Now, by introducing a third party into the customer conversation, both the customer and CEO get exactly what they need, namely, a candid conversation.

It's not a bait and switch, where subterfuge is used to bring customers out into the open so that a CEO can get a clear shot at them, because there's no guarantee that an acquisition will actually take place. The dialogue is focused on assessing and creating value—the value that's hidden from the balance sheet. The value that can only be measured by connecting with the customer.

The sales team will benefit. The customer service team will benefit. The executive leadership team will benefit.

Ideally, when it's done correctly, a third party uncovers issues and concerns that even customer-facing employees can't find. It's the marriage counselor principle at work: The right questions from the right party can lead to the right result. When you create an opportunity for everyone invested in the relationship to be heard, you can really get people talking.

What Bruce shared with me is what top CEOs know: Customer feedback is an opportunity to increase the valuation of your company. That value is there whether you are getting ready to sell or not. "In a sell situation, the buyer will want to know whether your customers are 'sticky.' In other words, are they going to stick with you in the coming months and years?" Bruce points out. "Some companies don't have an internal team that's focused on customer listening, so they hire us. And some companies say, 'Hey! We know our customers!' Except that they don't. We come in and bridge that knowledge gap."

A MATCH MADE IN HEAVEN

There are always things that can be better in any relationship. There are always surprises that a third party can uncover. Just ask any company that opened the Gartner Magic Quadrant and found themselves in a different box than they expected.

The "magic" of the Gartner Magic Quadrant (and similar analysis from other companies) is that Gartner analysts contact customers of companies they rate to get a third party, neutral view of what it's like to do business with a particular company.

For example, if you say that your products are great and easy to implement, and your customers say something else during the Gartner interviews, it changes the valuation of your company.

Keep in mind, sales teams and execs alike point to those third-party valuations in sales calls to differentiate themselves from competitors. And, because most customers view Gartner Magic Quadrant as a neutral data source, it holds weight.

There's always hidden value when you change who's asking the questions.

THE CUSTOMER EXPERIENCE ASSESSMENT

"CEOs who aren't necessarily determined to sell right now, but know that the day is coming, can invest in asking the right questions for the next three or four years. What they might spend to gather data with us is miniscule in comparison to what they will add in value to their company." In fact, the ROI can be 10x, 100x, or more, because the value of the customer set isn't a guess-timate. It's a clear report on the relationships and intentions that will drive future value.

The *Customer Experience Assessment* is like a balance sheet for your customer set. Beyond your company's bookkeeping processes is the real book of business: the intentions, actions, frustrations, and plans of your customers that paint a critical picture of your future. Bruce builds a business case for forward-thinking leaders, whether they actually end up selling or not, by gathering honest and unobstructed feedback: "It doesn't matter how good a company is or how well they take care of their clients. There are always surprises, things they can do better, things that are revealed when the right party asks the right questions around loyalty, intent, and commitment."

When buyers are evaluating an acquisition, they want to know the company's customers on a deeper level. Clear data leads to clear decisions; without input on customer loyalties, how can an investor assess the future value of the asset? More importantly, how can you present a business case that says, "This is what we're worth right now, and this is what we're going to be worth in the future"?

Maybe you don't care about forward-looking statements, the Magic Quadrant, and M&A work, but the value you create comes from one place: the customers who buy your product. This isn't a book about how to buy or sell a business, but it is a book about growth; about finding your way to new levels of financial health.

Can you ever know too much about your customers' wants and needs? What's the harm in evaluating your business as an investor would? In a buy/sell relationship, Bruce lets both companies know what they discover. When they find a surprise, like a repetitive software failure that hadn't been fully explored, it's shared with everyone. Why? So that a team of teams can get busy fixing it.

Here's how Bruce explains it: "I have three great kids. But every year—now that they're 33, 30, and 27—I learn stuff I kinda wish I didn't know. They tell me about things that were going on when they were 15, 12 and 9 and . . ." his voice trails off. He stops for a moment, tilting his head in the direction of the pictures on the shelf behind him, but he doesn't turn around. He blinks, takes a breath, and collects his thoughts. "I didn't know. Back then, I didn't know. And that didn't make me a bad parent. It just means that I wasn't aware. I didn't ask the right questions. That didn't mean I didn't care, I just didn't have the time or take the time or find the right words, I guess." The same thing happens in business.

"If I care about my customers," Bruce continues, "but I don't give them an opportunity to actually tell me what's going on from their perspective—not my perspective; if I don't give them an opportunity to share what's really important in our relationship . . . Well, what kind of a relationship do we really have?" Bruce asks.

C-Sparks: VoC Blackjack—a Quick Game of 21

Here are the 21 questions that KSM Consulting uses to help assess value in customer relationships for a fictitious company called OmniCorp. The key to this survey is to use it as a starting point—a place to begin the dialogue. Which questions look familiar? Which ones have a new context, and therefore a new meaning? "Be sure to mention," Bruce told me when he shared these details, "that these questions are not intended as an electronic survey or questionnaire. These are conversational prompts intended to be handled via a live conversation." From him to me to you, here's how that conversation shapes up:

SECTION I: PRODUCTS PURCHASED, COMPETITIVE LANDSCAPE, AND SHARE OF WALLET

Q1. Can you please provide some information about the kinds of products that OmniCorp provides you?

Q2. Can you share the reasons why you/your company selected Omni-Corp to provide those products?

Q3. What other suppliers with similar products to OmniCorp have you or do you purchase from as well?

Q4. How would you say that OmniCorp ranks in terms of your choice of a supplier?

    A. They are my first choice.

    B. They are the company I use if my preferred supplier cannot fulfill my needs.

    C. They are one of many suppliers that I use.

    D. Don't Know/Refused

Q5. On a scale from 1 to 5, with 1 being poor, 3 being average, and 5 being best of class, how would you rate/compare OmniCorp vs. Supplier 2 and Supplier 3 regarding:

    A. Product quality

    B. People/service

    C. Ease of doing business

    D. Pricing

Q6. How much of your purchasing volume (%) each year is typically sourced to OmniCorp? How has that amount changed over the past 1–2 years?

Q7. (If Share of Wallet is not 100%) Are there any issues or limitations that prevent OmniCorp from expanding their share of business with you?

Q8. Are there any new lines of products/services that OmniCorp can add that you would be interested in? Anything that you currently award to other suppliers because OmniCorp does not offer them today?

Q9. What would you say are OmniCorp's core competencies that differentiate them from the competition? What do they do really well or better than the competition?

Q10. What would you say are OmniCorp's biggest areas for improvement to better serve you?

SECTION II: LOYALTY METRICS AND PERFORMANCE ATTRIBUTES

The key to this section is to get commentary from the customer on why they rated OmniCorp as they did on each performance metric.

Q11. The next few questions will focus on how OmniCorp serves your needs. Based on all your experiences with OmniCorp, how would you rate their overall quality?

(*1–5 Poor to Excellent*)

Q12. How would you assess the value (price you pay vs. quality you get) that OmniCorp provides you? Would you say it is . . .

(*1–5 Poor to Excellent*)

Q13. Please tell me how much you agree with the following two statements:

A. I am committed to work with OmniCorp in the coming 1–2 years.

(*1–5 Strongly Disagree to Strongly Agree*)

B. It would matter a lot to me if I could not purchase from OmniCorp in the coming 1–2 years.

(*1–5 Strongly Disagree to Strongly Agree*)

(continued)

(continued)

Q14. How likely are you to continue awarding jobs to OmniCorp over the next 1–2 years?

(1–5 Not at All Likely to Extremely Likely)

Q15. What does the demand for your company's products look like in the coming 1–2 years? (Is this customer looking to grow? By extension, OmniCorp should have an opportunity to sell them more.)

(1–5 Decrease Substantially to Strongly Increase)

(Ask for percentages or actual projected numbers, as well as assumptions behind the growth or decline.)

Q16. Based on the demand for your products in the market, how much is your purchase volume with OmniCorp likely to change over the next 1–2 years?

(1–5 Decrease Substantially to Increase Substantially)

Q17. I would like to read a series of statements that could be used to describe OmniCorp. For each, please tell me the extent to which you agree with the statement.

(1–5 Strongly Disagree to Strongly Agree)

How would you rate OmniCorp on . . . ?

- Being easy to do business with
- Being a market leader
- Caring about its customers
- Having a strong, capable team
- Offering a wide range of products or capabilities
- Being a company I trust
- Being committed to getting the job done right

(Again, the key is to get each customer to share why they rated Omni-Corp as they did on each of these attributes, the "story" behind the rankings.)

Q18. Now I would like you to assess how OmniCorp works with your *organization.*

(1–5 Poor to Excellent)

How would you rate OmniCorp on . . . ?

- Communication/project planning
- Customer service and support

- Timely delivery/meeting deadlines
- Being available when you need them
- Ability to resolve problems that arise
- Being innovative—finding creative solutions
- Understanding your business needs

Q19. Next, I would like to ask you to assess OmniCorp's products using the same scale of

(1–5 Poor to Excellent)
- Being reliable/consistent
- Meeting your specifications
- Being best in class
- Being technologically advanced
- Being damage-free—no returns

Q20. Aside from price, what would you say are the top three factors that influence your company's purchasing decisions when it comes to products like OmniCorp offers?

Q21. This is our final question: Are there any open issues with OmniCorp or any feedback you would like to provide to OmniCorp's management team that might enhance your relationship with them?

BUILDING THE RELATIONSHIP

What if you could turn your customers into brand ambassadors for your company?

We all know the value in customer reviews in terms of brand-building. *Social Times* says that nearly 90 percent of people surveyed believe that customer reviews are the most effective content. Wendy Lea, Executive Chairman at GetSatisfaction in San Francisco (https://getsatisfaction.com/corp/), said at a recent CMO gathering, "The best thing we can do is lean in to the openness of customer conversations." https://bit.ly/listenup-cmogathering

Think about powerful consumer brands like Ducati motorcycles. The enthusiasts for these top-end Italian motorbikes are more than willing to engage in crosstalk and tips, especially if it means that they can be rewarded by the manufacturer. That reward doesn't necessarily come in the form of cash and prizes. Being on the inside track—and getting a backstage pass—can be its own reward. What would a backstage pass look like for your company's customers? Remember, what works for B2C can work for B2B as well.

At least, that's what Erica Kuhl (https://www.ericakuhl.com/) shared with me. As a consultant, she's helping companies to create authentic, engaged, and empowered communities. Ultimately, Erica helps companies to cultivate an environment in which shared experiences lead to competitive advantage.

We've already talked about the power of the backstage pass as it relates to customer advisory boards. But why stop there?

Giving customers a backstage pass (that feeling of exclusive access) within a context of shared experiences can create deeply loyal relationships. Erica puts that concept to work for her clients. She's discovered that customers who have a "backstage pass" love to share their insights with others. More than just bragging rights, these folks with something extra to share want to do so frequently and publicly, if there's a forum for that. In business, the backstage pass is a catalyst—it's the first step in creating change. When you pull customers closer to your company, you're taking the first step. Now you need a forum for the experience to grow and flourish. You can build an online community that helps people interact, solve problems for one another, and more. Here's how she pitched her first online community—a simple and powerful definition:

"The online community is a single hub for our customers to get their questions answered, to share their ideas, and to network with each other and with us."

Building a community gives your employees and your customers a place to belong. More importantly, Erica says, it brings your business a bigger pipeline, larger deals, higher adoption, lower attrition, and better customer service. In other words, expanding engagement is the key to expanding your value. And an online community is a great equalizer, taking ego out of the conversation and building an extended customer-centric culture. "My dream state," Erica shared with HuffPost (https://bit.ly/listenup-cmogathering), "for who should own the community is that it does not belong to ANY single department. It's like email—it's pervasive." The community belongs to the customers.

"Posting, voting, commenting, asking a question—that's where it all starts," Erica explains. "Customers like getting their questions answered fast by the community." The need to share expertise is built into the fabric of the Internet—the concept of sharing drives virtually every interactive social media website. Erica concludes, "Superusers like being able to share their expertise."

The key to the success of a customer community lies inside of its intention. If the community serves the customers, they will support it. However, if the community is built around serving the interests of the company, the program will never get off the ground. By offering real and authentic value, the community generates value for itself and, by extension, the company receives valuable insight, assistance, and guidance.

C-Sparks: Get Started Building Your Community

Seth Cohen writes in *Forbes* (https://bit.ly/listenup-cohen) that a customer community is the ultimate business interruption insurance: "When regular behaviors become irregular, customers who aren't part of a customer community become a lot less reliable. Conversely, customer communities rise up and deepen their commitment. Without a sense of being part of a community, customers use uncertain times to start to check out other businesses that offer the same goods and services but are closer or less expensive. For example, they might try new restaurants that have better pick-up or delivery options or fitness resources that have more effective online capabilities. The longer the interruption continues, the less connected they will be to your business's survival."

He goes on to say, "While customers might come and go, customer communities deepen and grow."

How do you begin building that community so that you can give your customers a sense of being part of a larger and more significant connection to your company while building new resources for them?

Here are the questions from Erica's feature story in HuffPost that can help you get started in building a brand community online:

- In what product/service areas can we create breakthrough, unique customer experiences?
- How would you rate the level of experience, market credentials, and passion for this particular product(s) or service(s) we are considering for the community?
- What are our objectives for creating a branded customer community (for example, gathering product feedback, handling complaints faster, solving problems collaboratively, celebrating successes, listening for new ideas, and so forth)?
- What is the size of our customer community today? Will 1 to 2 percent of that base be enough to launch and sustain ongoing customer conversations?
- How will we reward our top contributors or raving fans?

(continued)

(continued)

- What's our 12-month plan to grow customer engagement and commit to fast response times?
- How will we measure our success?
- Who will be accountable for our success?
- How will we ensure that our executive teams continue to listen and contribute to the community?

"You have to be able to produce data that shows the value of the community program," Erica elaborates. "Driving impact means taking a hard look at what the company's gaps are. For example, trying to get more customers, or keep customers longer, or scale, more sales, growth—it really comes down to one of these four or five big bucket areas for companies. If you want to create a community, align your program to one of those goals. Customer satisfaction is one you could align to, but be careful: CSAT has to be data-driven."

The company injects freedom and open communication into a community forum by design. But that doesn't mean that things turn into an online free-for-all. Strategic leaders are listening, monitoring, and watching, identifying trends and measuring success. "You can't do CSAT (customer satisfaction) surveys right out of the gate. The customers will feel it—feel that you're doing this community for yourself, not for their success," Erica confirms.

How can you engage your customers in helping each other? Rather than shelling out surveys, start monitoring and measuring top topics in the discussion forums. Find ways to empower your power-users to help those who are new to your products. Pull those power-users closer than ever: Give them insight into product development, updates, and proposed initiatives. You don't have to share the recipe for Diet Coke or some other closely guarded corporate secret. But offering insight into the inside of your company is how you create stark raving fans. Can you pull back the curtain, just a little, so that your best customers gain an inside perspective? With insight comes support. You build a base of customers that extends your brand—even extending your first-level tech support in some cases—and leveraging the expertise outside of your company.

What would it mean to you if you could turn your customers into brand advocates? How would that add value to your organization, your brand, your overall market value? Could it even reduce the burden on your customer service team?

COMMUNITY KILLS COMPETITION

Involvement and engagement are within your reach. "One of the most powerful human emotions," Erica says simply, "is a sense of belonging."

When you create a community, you create expansive brand value. You leverage your greatest assets—your customers—to create a competitive powerhouse.

When it comes to customer listening, look who's talking. Don't wait to get customers talking to each other. Bring in third-party expertise—resources from outside of your own company—if you want to hear what you would otherwise miss. Turning your customers into advocates, via community forums, accelerates the customer's journey.

Now it's time to look at how that journey can come together. We've looked at the questions and the questioner, so that you can drive exceptional value. Build community. Expand your brand. Next up, we'll consider the right time for transformation, and we'll look at how you can put new ideas into action.

CHAPTER 15

Moment of Signal

My silver-haired doctor had just told me he knew what was wrong with me. He knew what we needed to do. The news was good. Why was I still looking at the floor?

"Karen. How are you doing?" he asked.

Barefoot on the examination table, the answer wasn't so simple for me. Hope was the one thing I wanted. And the one thing I feared I would never find. Was this it, I wondered? Can I trust what this guy is saying? On the shiny counter to my left, there was a plastic rack of pamphlets on diabetes, heart disease, and mental health. Comfort for the pain. My answers weren't in that rack. I needed a cure, not a brochure.

I've tried everything, I thought to myself. Is this conversation really any different? How will I find what's missing? How can I filter out the noise to know that what he's saying is really an answer I can believe in?

Pleasantries and common answers were nowhere to be found. Saying "I'm fine" would be a lie and a waste of time. My voice was hoarse, and my answer was raw.

"I feel . . . hopeless," I said.

In that moment, the normal rapid fire cadence of my life slowed to a standstill. My breathing was shallow. A sharp intake of air took me by surprise, like the start of a laugh but different. Isn't it funny how tears and laughter can start from the same place? The deep green and blue fibers in the shorthaired carpet started to blur out of focus. Water covered the world. The tears had come again, and I had no way to stop them.

In front of me, the man in the lab coat stood up. Patient and waiting, he placed a hand on my shoulder.

"I hear you," he said.

A Kleenex box was lifted in my general direction. Once again, my doc had exactly what I needed.

I still didn't know whether he had the correct diagnosis. But I didn't need to know that right now. Because, in those three words, I found hope: "I hear you." In that moment, I found the treatment that I needed most.

RESTORING HOPE

In the middle of a challenge, whether it's a health crisis or an impossible business obstacle, people need to be heard. Listened to. Understood.

More important than a diagnosis or a treatment plan is that moment of signal: the signal that says, "I hear you."

Connection is what restores hope. Connection to the understanding that you don't have to go it alone. The understanding that together, we can find new solutions.

Do your customers know that you are paying attention? Do your customers know that you want to partner with them in deeper and more powerful ways, where you create a shared agenda that's focused on their success?

Listening, I have found, is the most powerful tool in business today. Your customers are looking for hope. For answers. For guidance. And for products and services that can help them to build (or rebuild) their impact.

There's a lot of noise out there: misdiagnoses, misunderstanding, and misdirection. How can your customers know who to turn to?

They turn to the partner who says, "I hear you. I hear you in ways that others don't, or won't, or can't." The partner who's willing to listen.

The source of direction, guidance, and new results is the voice of the customer. Listen for it. Be the resource that your customers need.

Let your customers know that you hear them. Let your team know the same. Invite candor into the conversation and uncover the barriers to value. Connection. New results.

It's easy to see the competition as some other company or alternative solution. No matter who you're fighting, the best way to compete is by building the strongest team. Are you teaming up with your customers right now? I bet they could use your help. Here's how to start.

C-Sparks: Guideposts and Goalposts

If you want an easy way to remember the steps in creating greater relationships, partnerships, and profits, all you have to do is *Listen Up!*

L *"Look for the lead domino."* Where's the true customer here? The one that's going to create the greatest impact? How can you use live listening to find what's missing?

I Ignite your genius. You can stop asking yesterday's questions as soon as you are ready. Look for your genius and make it easier for everyone to do business with you. Whether that's your largest customer, or your smallest STAR account, your A-Game is as close as one new idea.

S Suspend your preconceptions. Start with a beginner's mind. The conversation really gets interesting when you realize that you don't know, but you want to find out. Look closely at what it is you think you already know. And then, realize that you don't. There's always more to discover when you start with a beginner's mind.

T Test your hypothesis. Take a pause. *Test* your ideas. Like a scientist, you start an experiment with a beginner's mind. Perhaps you have a theory or two about the customer journey. Just remember, the map is not the territory. In person, Colorado looks very different than it does on my GPS. So too is the customer journey. It can't be discovered on a whiteboard or a map. You have to see it, hear it, and experience it for yourself. Test, try, and test again. Look for micro-moments to influence the relationship. Detach from the outcome so that you can truly listen. Whether your hypothesis is right or wrong, what you observe, hear, and learn is *always* a great result, because what you learn informs your next step! At the end of the day, it's not about being right—it's about being informed!

E Empower every employee to act, to swarm the customer, and to marshal the resources needed to get to the right answer. My doctor was kind enough to listen, but he didn't stop there. He put together a plan—a plan that empowered me to take back my life. If you care about conquering your competition, make your team stronger. If you want to make miracles happen, give your team of miracle workers what they need, whether that's technology, tools, or a culture that focuses on what really matters, empowerment is the only way to turn listening into action.

N Neutralize ego. Who do you want to win in the battle for the customer? Your agenda or your company? The path to the beginner's mindset requires that you neutralize ego. Get rid of the need to be right, and you're headed in the right direction. If you're focused on yourself, your agenda, and your fiefdom, where's the customer in that conversation? You've got the Secret Sauce; don't let ego ruin what's cooking.

U Use stories with statistics. Numbers are points in a narrative; they never tell the whole story. What's the story behind the score? What's the conversation behind the customer analysis? Spreadsheets support

(continued)

(continued)

the story, but they can't speak for themselves. That's why you have to. You have to provide the insights that make the information meaningful. Relevant. Relatable. Don't bet on a single number—it's just too risky. Share stories in the language of the C-Suite: Look in the direction of impact, outcomes, and results.

P People before process. Any tools that you use now or acquire in the future are designed to serve your people—either your employees or your customers or both. Whatever digital trends emerge and whatever online strategies come to the forefront, remember that a tool is only as good as the people who use it. If you set up a sophisticated AI around rudimentary questions, your tech tools won't teach you a thing. Always consider the people at the center of any process. Design and align that process around the folks who will benefit most from it, creating a culture in which every employee is empowered to serve the customer. Don't let technology drive your decisions. Make wise choices for people first, and invest in the technology that supports your vision.

When I knew my doctor had heard me, I knew that my concerns around hopelessness were ok. I knew that I wasn't alone. I knew that my doctor was as invested in my success as I was, because I felt *heard*.

And because he took action. From that first prescription to our final treatment, he was looking in the direction of my health and well-being.

But before I began gaining my life back, before I started fighting my way back to normal, there was one vital element that I had to embrace.

I had to trust.

I'm not talking about trusting in myself, or even believing in my doctor. Because, when someone says, "Believe in yourself," which self do they mean? The successful author self? The TEDx speaker self? Or the self that nearly got fired for a fouled-up fumble in a meeting in Louisville? The self that burned the soufflé and spilled the coffee? Or the self that can fall prey to some mysterious disease? How about the version of myself that read a sales report to a customer in a dusty forgotten office complex, hoping for the best?

As they say, everywhere you go there you are. Good and bad. Success and failure. Through it all, here's what I learned:

Moods don't create results. If I had to trust in myself—the self that was riddled with a mysterious illness—I never would have made it. Because I couldn't. I *couldn't* trust in myself. At first, I didn't even trust my doctor. But that didn't mean I was stuck.

I had to trust in the one thing that matters more than mindset. I had to trust in *taking action*.

I stepped off the examination table and felt the fibers of the carpet beneath my feet. I smoothed my skirt, pushed back my hair, dried my cheeks. The doctor was writing a new prescription with his silver pen. Our appointment was over, but I wasn't finished trying to find my way back to health.

If you want to redefine yourself after a health crisis, trust in your own understanding. Trust in the knowledge of what Isaac Newton told us. That thing that you know to be true: *for every action there is an equal and opposite reaction*.

What would have happened if I had stopped to manage my mindset? What if I waited until I could trust myself before I moved forward? I didn't feel great, it's true, but I didn't feel like giving up, either.

Like the hockey players on Herb Brooks's miracle team, I got back out on the ice. I started moving, trying, exploring, and doing. His weird quote, "Legs feed the wolf," finally made sense: The wolf has to keep moving! No matter what your mood: Keep. Moving. Forward.

Progress always comes in motion. My emotions came and went, and it was quite a roller coaster, as I'm sure you can imagine. When I did what I needed to do, even if it was difficult, actions led to reactions. Reactions led to results. As I look back on it, action led me to this doctor, this tiny office, this simple three-word conversation: "I hear you."

Finding normal, for me, was a journey. And like every journey, it started when I put one foot in front of the other; when I looked at the principles and ideas that had been offered to help me to find a new way, a new way home.

When I started writing this book, people were taking meetings in restaurants, going to conventions, and traveling on airplanes. As I close this chapter, we are not. As you read these words, I can't begin to guess what the world looks like for you.

How can I say something timely in a way that fits for *your* time? I have to look to what I know to be true, regardless of your circumstances or mine.

Whether you are in a doctor's office, a company office, or your home office, here's what I know beyond a shadow of a doubt:

Listening is where powerful stories begin.

Want to start a powerful dialogue? Let your customers know that they are heard—that someone is listening. Someone is invested in their success. Because if you don't, your competition will.

When I left my doctor's office, I knew that I never wanted my health to go back to where it was before. I wanted something new. Something better. I'm guessing that if you've made it this far, you want those things, too. Are you ready to walk away from what you've always done if it's not getting you the results you want?

What about those results? If you're looking for new ways to put listening into action, and you want to redefine customer success, I can help. If your organization is looking for fresh ideas, *I hear you*. Reach out to me at http://karenmangia.com and share your story.

Uncertainty will always be with us. But you can trust in this principle, like the law of gravity, because it always works: ***Action creates results***.

What action could we take together? The customer conversation is the action that matters most. New results begin when you Listen Up! And I want to hear from you.

Now you know how to ask better questions, create greater alignment, build value, and share your genius beyond the survey. Trust in what you've read and learned. Trust in what you've discovered as you've taken your own journey through these pages. But ultimately, turn that trust into action.

Because that's when the story really gets interesting.

About the Author

Karen Mangia is Vice President, Customer and Market Insights, at Salesforce and Chair of the Customer Experience Council for The Conference Board. An internationally recognized thought leader in Voice of the Customer (VOC), Customer Experience (CX), and Customer Success, Karen's keynotes and TEDx talks reach hundreds of thousands of business leaders each year. She is the recipient of the Distinguished Alumni Award from Ivy Tech Community College, Hall of Fame and Graduate of Distinction from Ball State University, and 40 Under 40 from the *Indianapolis Business Journal*. She is also a professionally trained chef. Her first book, *Success With Less: Releasing Obligations and Discovering Joy*, was published in 2016. Her second book, *Working from Home: Making the New Normal Work for You*, was published in 2020.

Learn more by connecting with her at http://karenmangia.com.

Acknowledgments

*L*isten Up! resulted from talented and otherwise busy people who went from interested to invested. To those who never wavered in their support, I am deeply grateful. To the generous collaborators who opened doors, removed roadblocks, and made this story come alive, you are the reason why this book is here.

My thanks to Bruce Richardson for suggesting that I write this book and for acting as a one-person research arm in the months that followed. Your statistics, stories, and support provided a firm foundation on which to build a compelling case for change. Your red wine and your listening ear made the tough days better. I toast you.

To Tony Rodoni, John Stormer, and John Taschek for believing in this message and for acting as Executive Sponsors in word and in deed. Your investment created momentum and unlocked doors that might otherwise have been bolted shut. Thank you to Anne Chen, Deb Ho, Teresa Soriano, Michelle Balbi, and JT Garnett for navigating the path to get the right resources in the right place at the right time. And to Warren Wick and Thanhia Sanchez for your expert introductions and collaboration.

My colleagues smoothed the path, allowing me to share the story beyond the survey. Dan Farber—you made the original proposal and the subsequent manuscript better. And to David Simon, Joe Olsen, and April Oliver for your partnership in maintaining the integrity of our company and our customers throughout this journey and beyond.

Trailblazers are the innovators who go first and who make the way easier for others. My thanks to the following authors: Chris O'Hara, *Data Driven: Harnessing Data and AI to Reinvent Customer Engagement* (McGraw-Hill Education, 2018), Mathew Sweezey, *The Context Marketing Revolution: How to Motivate Buyers in the Age of Infinite Media* (Harvard Business Review Press 2020), and Tiffani Bova, *Growth IQ: Get Smarter About the Choices That Will Make or Break Your Business* (Portfolio/Penguin, 2018) for your encouragement and your expertise. You were generous with your templates, your time, your lessons learned, and your connections.

Collaborating with Geoffrey Moore, a career bucket list experience, was made possible through the generosity of Jay Thayer and the guidance of Josh Aranoff. Geoff, the power of your belief in the timeliness and relevance of the concepts in this book ignited a fiery passion to dig deeper, reach higher, and stretch further in order to imagine the future and to challenge the status quo. Thank you for sharing your brilliant insights in the foreword, even though your dance card is plenty full already.

I would not be where I am today without Chris Westfall. Your coaching helped me find my voice when writing *Success With Less: Releasing Obligations and Discovering Joy* (Marie Street Press, 2016), which set the stage for this book. Thank you for elevating my practitioner's speech, shaping my stories, and making sure that the reader was at the center of every word, tip, and takeaway. Thank you for taking my late-night phone calls, for listening to my crazy ideas (without ever calling them crazy), for making this journey fun, and for knowing just when I needed to press pause and change the channel. You have a gift. You are a gift. I'm grateful that you were willing to join me on this adventure.

The team at Wiley is exceptional. Thank you to Jeanenne Ray, Sally Baker, and the entire team for your responsiveness and your guidance. And to Gary Schwartz for your editorial expertise. I value the relationship we've built and what we've produced together.

Thank you to the companies and subject-matter experts who trusted me with your stories: Christi Hill at Eli Lilly, Chris Chapman at Google, Christine Marcus at Alchemista, Eelco Thiellier at Royal Haskonnig, Katherine Mosquera, Tom Boyd, and Kevin Hickey at Maersk, Russ Wilson at Fidelity, and Yana Kakar at Dalberg. I owe a debt of gratitude to Brian Solis, Ray Wang, Erica Kuhl, Bruce Kidd, and Amy Brown for articulating a path to the future. And to Lauren Culbertson, Jane Riad, John Adams, John Bannister, Brent Clodgo, Vince DeLuca, Renae Johnson, Tom Grothues, and Ed Frampton, whose expertise proved invaluable in shaping the best practices shared within this book.

Sunday afternoons are special to me because I'm treated to one beer, one cup of coffee, and one steak the size of a dinner plate with my grandfather (who still cooks!) and my aunt. The outpouring of wisdom, love, and support that spans those afternoons is what I savor most. Grandpa: Remember the iPad I promised for your 100th birthday.

The only reason why there's coffee in my pantry and dry cleaning in my closet is because my mom rearranged her life to support mine. Thank you.

Lorelei, Piper, and Brynn, you are my joy and my heart. My grandmother told me that she understood true love the first time she looked into my newborn eyes. And I feel the same way about each of you. Thank you for your box of letters—I will treasure them for life. You are proof that love conquers all, and you remind me of what matters most in life.

Friends are the family we choose. To Renee for teaching me the ins and outs of the publishing industry, making introductions, and opening first growth champagne when needed. To Andrew for reminding me what a gift this opportunity represents and for being with me every step of the way. To John, Michael, Lady T, BDJ, and Jill for feeding my body and my soul along the way—and for the impromptu, fun distractions.

Last and not least to Eric. For never once lamenting the downgrade from carbonara to carry out. For saying, "I'm so proud of you. You can do this," every single day. For playing video clips to make me laugh. For sacrificing time together to make room for this project. And for pretending that this book is a revelation, even though you could probably quote it word for word.

Finally, to all my readers. I wrote this story to let you know that you're not alone, and to offer you the tools to design the future for and with your customers. Success is yours when you have the courage to Listen Up!

—Karen Mangia

Index

resolving complaints, 90
resources, for transforming customer experience/support, 93
retail customers, personalization and, 44
retention, 12
Return on Insights (ROI), 43
Revell, Ashley, 9–11
reviewing
  customer comments, 41
  recognition programs, 41
  rewards programs, 41
rewards
  reviewing programs, 41
  for success, 43
ROI (Return on Insights), 43
Rometty, Ginni (CEO), 64
Roosevelt, Eleanor, 6
Royal HaskoningDHV, 53, 54
rules, genius and, 79

S

Salesforce, 5, 39, 44, 60, 66, 79–80
Saudi Arabia, 130
Schiphol Airport, 52
Secret Sauce
  C-Sparks, 102–103, 105, 107–108
  ego, 100, 107–108
  example of, 97–100
  necessity *vs.* ease, 100–109
  presentation tips, 105
  surveys, 102–103
security, false sense of, 23–25
seeking, intentionally, 138
Segall, Laurie, 80
selection bias, 132
self-describing, 30
senior leaders, choosing to do customer follow-up, 18–19
service issues, examples of, 83–87
serving

charging for your services, 43
  at higher levels, 4
  before speaking, 108
share of wallet, assessing value in customer relationships using, 146–147
sharing customer metrics with customers, 41
shifting focus, 108
signal
  connection restoring hope, 156–160
  C-Sparks, 156–158
  example of, 155–156
silos, for feedback, 107
Sinek, Simon, 116
Skype, 45
Smart Think (website), 60
snap judgment, 133
Solis, Brian, 127, 135–137, 139–140
  Lifescale: How to Live a More Creative, Productive, and Happy Life, 136
  WTF?: What's the Future of Business?: Changing the Way Businesses Create Experiences, 136
  X: The Experience When Business Meets Design, 136
solutions
  process as, 96
  values and, 136–138
solving complexity, 76
South Africa, 63
strategic visions, 39
Stuart, Anthony, 71–74
Stuart, Marion, 71
Stuart's Moving and Storage, 71–74
success, recognizing and rewarding, 43